Eat Smart
IN
FRANCE

Eat Smart IN FRANCE

How to Decipher the Menu
Know the Market Foods
&
Embark on a Tasting Adventure

Ronnie Hess

GINKGO PRESS INC

Madison, Wisconsin

Map lettering is by Gail L. Carlson; cover and insert photographs are by Ronnie Hess except
for the insert photograph of the "pigeon heart" tomatoes, which was by Sara Patterson;
author photograph is by Del Brown.

The quote by James A. Michener from "This Great Big Wonderful World," from the March
1956 issue of Travel-Holiday Magazine, © 1956 by James A. Michener, is reprinted by
permission of William Morris Endeavor Entertainment on behalf of the author.

Publisher's Cataloging-in-Publication
(Provided by Quality Books Inc.)
Hess, Ronnie
    Eat smart in France : how to decipher the menu, know
the market foods & embark on a tasting adventure /
Ronnie Hess
    p. cm.
    Includes bibliographical references and index.
    LCCN: 2010926427
    ISBN-13: 978-0-9776801-2-2
    ISBN-10: 0-9776801-2-6

    1. Cooking, French. 2. Diet--France. 3. Food habits
--France. 4. France--Guidebooks. 5. France--
Description and travel. I. Title.

TX719.H47 2010   641.5944
                    QBI10-600130

Printed in the United States of America

In memory of my parents,

who always had Paris

Contents

Shopping in France's Food Markets   69

Tips to increase your savvy in both the exciting outdoor food markets and modern supermarkets.

Resources   71

A listing of stores carrying hard-to-find French foods, and groups offering opportunities for person-to-person contact through home visits to gain a deeper understanding of the country, including its cuisine.

Helpful Phrases   75

Phrases in English translated to French, with additional phonetic interpretation, which will assist you in finding, ordering and buying foods or ingredients.

Menu Guide   79

An extensive listing of menu entries in French, with English translations, to make ordering food an easy and immediately rewarding experience.

Foods and Flavors Guide   105

A comprehensive glossary of ingredients, kitchen utensils and cooking methods in French, with English translations.

Food Establishments   135

A quick reference guide to restaurants and shops visited.

Preface

> If you reject the food, ignore the customs, fear the religion and avoid the people, you might better stay home. You are like a pebble thrown into water; you become wet on the surface but you are never a part of the water.
> —JAMES A. MICHENER

I fell in love with French cooking at the tender age of ten. A French classmate had invited me for lunch one Sunday and it was in her family's dining room that I met two dishes that would change my outlook on life. One was a potato gratin brought to the table bubbling with cream. The other was a *gâteau Saint-Honoré,* a complicated dessert of cream puffs, pastry cream and caramelized sugar. Although I didn't completely understand it at the time, the meal taught me something essential about French cooking. It was nothing less than golden—it inspired the eye, it satisfied the palate. It nourished body and soul.

Food at my house had not conveyed that kind of grace or glamour. My mother was working full-time and going to college. Dinners *chez nous* were pretty straightforward—the usual dishes were meatloaf or chicken cooked in a pressure cooker along with a can of cream of celery soup. But my mother, born in England of Dutch immigrant parents, had been brought up understanding the importance of cooking with the seasons, and of using almost all parts of an animal. She wasn't squeamish when it came to organ meat—she loved brains, calf's liver and kidneys. She also had a great fondness, as did my German-Jewish father, for French food.

My parents had met in Paris on a blind date one Sunday morning in April, and it was love at first sight. One thing led to another over breakfast and, since it was my father's birthday, they decided to see each other again that evening. My mother would always recollect what she ordered for dinner—lobster and wild strawberry tart.

Years later, when we traveled across France as a family, I remember her buying young, thin green beans at the market and smuggling them on the car ferry across the Channel to her sisters in England. And there were many other moments, such as the night when she was staying with me in Paris and I came home from work to a pot of bubbling rabbit stew. She also discovered the butcher shop that specialized in horsemeat.

Let it also be said that my father was a bon vivant, whose passion was desserts, in particular Sacher-Torte and strawberry cheesecake. My parents' culinary culture wars—and they were fierce—were usually fought over meat and vegetables. My mother liked hers undercooked, my father his well-done. Toward the end of the meal, she usually brought out a cheese and fruit plate but my father always insisted on something sweet.

Although I took cooking classes from a French chef in the 1970s and was one of Julia Child's millions of fans, it was during my years traveling around France that I came to have a deeper appreciation of French culture and French cooking. Like Muriel Barbery's food critic in *Gourmet Rhapsody,* food memories linger—the supper in a small restaurant next door to Rouen's youth hostel when I was in my early twenties—a bowl of vegetable soup (*potage*), a slice of ham, a salad. Or, again in Rouen, when I was a little older, raw oysters redolent of the sea; or the majestic *soufflé Grand Marnier* one summer afternoon in Brittany; or roast chicken flavored with cognac in Honfleur. I realized that the best French cooking didn't have to be complicated or mannered. At its best, it could be simple, honest, delectable—the best ingredients, prepared well, dishes savored leisurely with friends.

It was the same when I lived in Paris for several years working as a reporter for CBS News. There were occasional dinners in Michelin-starred restaurants but more frequently inexpensive meals (usually sausage) in the bistro around the corner; the flakiest croissants from a shop along the rue Marbeuf; or Saturday and Sunday mornings meandering through outdoor markets, and reading the newspaper in a café over a steaming cup of *grand crème;* or dinners and picnics with family and friends on weekends in Paris but also special places—the hills above St. Tropez (olives); a backyard in the middle of Normandy (bread and cheese); a house in the Dordogne (wild mushrooms sautéed in butter). Years later, I thought I had gone to heaven one rainy night at a *table d'hôte* near Toulouse where the innkeeper served my husband and me foie gras and grilled lamb chops—*produits de la ferme*—from animals raised on his farm.

You might think that given this background I would know all about French cuisine. But researching this book has been a humbling experience. Despite all my travels, and my own cooking, I have realized there is always much to learn. France is a large, bountiful and complicated country. Food practices have developed and changed over hundreds, maybe even thousands, of years. There are particular local customs, special regional dishes, and variations in food preparations from one place to another. The ingredients in a *cassoulet* in Castelnaudary may be different from those a few miles down the road in Carcassonne. In addition, methods of food production are changing, along with increasing standardization and industry concentration.

No cuisine ever stays the same, even in France where haute cuisine was born. Young French chefs are playing with new ingredients, experimenting with different tastes and combinations. There are new international influences and alterations in French lifestyles and work habits. Factor in as well health concerns surrounding consumption of excess animal fats that are giving olive oil a big boost in parts of the country where butter used to be king. And yet, one senses there is continuity, that there is still something quintessentially French in France's food.

No book about French cooking can ever hope to be comprehensive but it's my hope that this one will be a good companion, answering both practical questions, such as how to figure out a menu and how to shop, as well as more substantial ones dealing with culinary history. The book is designed for all readers, for those who are just starting to adventure into French cooking and the more seasoned traveler.

As with other books in the EAT SMART series, there are four main chapters. The first provides a brief history of French cuisine; the second takes readers around the country with descriptions of regional foods. Other main chapters provide extensive menu listings and a glossary of terms associated with the preparation and serving of food, arranged alphabetically. They are at the back of the book for easy reference. Some of the menu items are labeled "national favorite" and "regional classic" in the margins next to the entry. As with a travel guide, this is a way to key the reader to dishes that are "worth the detour," or not to be missed.

There is more practical information in chapters offering hints on browsing and shopping France's food markets, and featuring phrases that may be useful as you visit markets, shops and restaurants. There is a chapter of recipes tested in EAT SMART's kitchens, ones you can try any time, either before setting off for France or on your return. The recipes come from a variety of sources and represent different kinds of cooking. You'll find instructions for preparing regional dishes such as a rice pudding from Normandy and sweet yeast bread from the Dauphiné. Included, too, are classic French dishes, such as *bœuf bourguignon* and *vichyssoise,* as well as riffs on regional favorites such as *pissaladière,* a tomato and red pepper tart from southern France. The recipes come from chefs and home cooks, new friends and old who are devoted to French cooking, whether they were born or chose to live in France.

French cuisine has become so popular around the world that most ingredients in these recipes can be obtained in the United States. Where special ingredients are called for, substitutions are suggested. Sources for French foodstuffs can be found in the chapter on resources, which also cites groups that focus on travel to France, with opportunities to gain a deeper understanding of the country and its cuisine.

As you set off on your French adventure, here are a few additional thoughts. Don't be afraid to go off the beaten track (provided that it's safe to do so). You may discover something remarkable and memorable in the unlikeliest places, such as that farm not far from Toulouse. Be curious and ask questions. Many French people speak English and are happy to converse. And don't be squeamish—be ready to savor new tastes. Finally, enthusiasm and respect go a long way in a foreign country, and *merci* is one of the best words to know.

RONNIE HESS
Madison, Wisconsin

Acknowledgments

I would like to gratefully acknowledge many people who assisted in making this book possible.

Colette Friedlander was especially helpful in filling in many blanks and for assistance with translation and editing; Yvonne Schofer and Catherine Bonnard Sullivan edited the *Menu Guide* and *Foods & Flavors Guide;* Lynn Courtenay, University of Wisconsin–Whitewater Emerita Professor of Art History, and Jean Vaché offered important suggestions to chapters on culinary history and regional foods. My thanks go to Susan Chwae of Ginkgo Press for cover design and illustrations; Sara Patterson for additional photographs; Brook Soltvedt for scrupulous editing; and recipe-testing friends in my international book group.

Special recognition goes to those who welcomed me into their kitchens and shops: Catherine and Patrick Auduc (La Vieille Auberge, Saulieu); Calvados maker Marie Bourut (Manoir du Val, Saint-Aubin-le-Guichard); chef David Brochet (Le Rouennais, Rouen); chocolatier Christian Constant (Christian Constant, Paris); André Daguin, former owner-chef of Hotel de France in Auch, his daughters Anne Daguin (La Grande Duchesse, Paris) and Ariane Daguin (D'Artagnan, Newark, New Jersey); chef François Deduit and his wife Edwige (Hostellerie du Moulin Fouret, Saint-Aubin-le-Vertueux); chef Stéphane Derbord and his wife Isabelle (Restaurant Stéphane Derbord, Dijon); Nathalie and Marc Désarménien (La Moutarderie Fallot, Beaune); proprietors Bernard and Joëlle Dubreuil, their daughter Cécile and cuisinier Jean Evenas (Les Routiers, Paris); Madeleine Gossent (La Londe Bed and Breakfast, near Heudreville-sur-Eure); seed savers Frédéric Lamblin, Natacha Levasseur and Armelle Viallon (Potager de Beaumesnil); author Susan Loomis (On Rue Tatin Cooking School, Louviers); Calvados maker Etienne Luroy (Cellier Clos du Bourg, Saint-Saire); beekeepers Florent and Mélanie Maugeais (Les Ruchers de Normandie, Le Bosc-Roger, near Gisay-la-Coudre); chef Frédéric Ménager and his wife Eva (La Ferme de la Ruchotte, near Bligny-sur-Ouche); Laurent Moinet (La Ferme de Hyaumet, Dampierre-en-Bray); Catherine Petitjean-Dugourd (La Maison Mulot & Petitjean, Dijon); Apollonia Poilâne (Poilâne, Paris), her assistant Geneviève Briere and Olivier Beslay (La Cuisine de Bar, Paris); chef Bridget Pugh (La Terrasse du Mimosa, Montpeyroux); chef Patrick Ramelet (Auberge du Beau-Lieu, Le Fossé, near Forges-les-Eaux); chef Didier Robert and his mother Colette (Le Piano Qui Fume, Dijon); chef Peter Shaw and his wife Sally (Here on the Spot catering and gourmet holidays, Quarante); author Brigitte Tilleray; Erick Vedel (Provence Cooks, Arles); and Blandine and Pascale Zoutard (La Ferme de Saint-Mamert, Buis-sur-Damville).

Others who were generous with their time explaining the fine points of French cuisine were: artist Françoise Calisti, who offers occasional cooking classes in Paris; Mary Ann Caws, Distinguished Professor, the Graduate School of the City University of New York; Sylvère Gonzalvez (Terroir Direct, Montpellier); Steven L. Kaplan, Professor of History, Cornell University; Colette and Pierre Manin in Peyrins; their niece, Joëlle Manin; Bernadette and Eric Maréjus in Dijon; Françoise and Gilles Peyrat in Dijon; Slow Food France members Jérôme Duval, Lolo Fermont, Mickaël and Marie-Pierre Jammes, Christophe Lançon and Remy Lemonnier; Dominique Vaché in Clapiers; retired pastry chef Lionel Varin and his wife Marie-France in Hauville.

Special thanks also to those who shared useful contacts and information: Randall Berndt; Stéphane Grynszpan; Michael Hinden and Betsy Draine; Andrew Jefford; John Kuony and Suzanne Kuony Smack; Sylvie Manin; Henrik Mattsson; Jane Schulenburg; Soyo Graham Stuart and Karl Horwitz; Dominique Taquet; Ann Topham (Fantôme Farm, Ridgeway, WI); Amy Trubek; Madeleine Vedel; Stuart Whatling; the staff of the University of Wisconsin–Madison Memorial Library's Special Collections, Birge Library and the Chazen Museum of Art, Madison, WI. Thanks also go to Anne Flouest (Bibracte Museum), Bérengère Foyard (Institut Paul Bocuse), Martine Bocuse and Pierre Bocuse.

There are also French friends from years ago whose influence is still keenly felt, including Charles Mazières and the late Jean Vieuchange and his family.

Special thanks go to Ginkgo Press publisher Joan Peterson whose belief in this project never wavered, and to my sister, Sally, for her unfailing support.

Finally, I am fortunate to have in my husband, Ron Rosner, a seasoned traveler, excellent editor and all-around good sport.

Eat Smart

IN

FRANCE

MAP OF FRANCE

The Cuisine of France

An Historical Survey

For generations, the food of France has been synonymous with the elegance and artistry of haute cuisine; and with a more modest but traditional and regional home cookery, *la cuisine bourgeoise*. Today, these distinctions may no longer be helpful. French cooking is in flux, but not for the first time. France's history has been punctuated by foreign invasion, war, pestilence, New World exploration, feast and famine, colonial conquest, revolution, occupation and immigration. During these times, new foods from all corners of the world and cross-cultural exchanges have left their mark on French eating and entertaining and have created a culinary pattern of change.

Early Beginnings

In September 1940, a group of French teenagers went for a hike in the Périgourdine hills of central France. They knew that many years before, stones with prehistoric carvings had been uncovered in the area. The teens were keen to discover their own buried treasure. What they stumbled upon at Lascaux exceeded their wildest expectations—a cave filled with marvelous wall paintings of ancient horses and bulls. Discoveries in other caves followed, along with a greater appreciation of the art and archaeology of peoples dwelling here some 40,000 years ago. Thanks to these cave painters we can get a glimmer of early life in the country that would become France.

During the Ice Age, France was a land populated by small groups of hunter-gatherers, no more than 5,000 individuals in all. Plants were their most significant food source, but there was also game. Reindeer probably provided most of the animal protein but there was a profusion of animal life to feed the inhabitants. As Gregory Curtis points out in his delightful book,

The Cave Painters, "every species native to Europe today was there, along with species that are now extinct"—hedgehogs, shrews, moles, rats, mice and other rodents, minks, ermines, badgers, otters, wolves, jackals, foxes and raccoons. Human diets may have included hyenas, wolverines, cave lions and cave bears, as well as woolly mammoths, polecats, lynx, small-headed leopards and cheetahs, who in turn stalked elk, aurochs and other large game. Ice Age hunters ate eggs and small birds, partridge and grouse. They caught fish with thorns and, later, more-sophisticated hooks made of bone and horn. Other foodstuffs included leaves, nettles and ferns; root vegetables such as turnips and radishes; grains; fruits; bulbs, such as onions; and mushrooms. Most likely, marrow was consumed almost raw; crushed bones probably were used to make a watery soup heated over stones.

By 7000 BCE, as knowledge of plant and animal domestication spread across Europe from the Middle East, pastoral communities sprouted up. Goats, sheep, pigs and cows were managed. Crops included early varieties of wheat (emmer and einkorn) and barley. Weeds such as rye and oats, which thrived in cooler climates, were domesticated. Pulses or dried legumes, poppy and flax were grown as well. Forests still provided significant foodstuffs, especially acorns, which could be ground into flour. There were wild fruits to pick, including apples, plums and raspberries; onions, nettles, dandelions, sorrel and goosefoot to pluck up; snails to grab and varieties of fresh- and saltwater fish to snare. Flints, scrapers, grinders, sickles, polished stones for axheads, wicker baskets and fish traps were common tools. Clay pots were limited in number and quality but still did the job, storing foodstuffs and serving as cooking vessels. Meats were stewed, grilled, smoked and cooked in pits.

The Greeks, the Romans, the Gauls

By 2000 BCE, merchants sailing the waters of the Mediterranean were hawking new foodstuffs. The Greeks brought wine to France in exchange for a variety of goods, grain being among the most important, as the fertility of lands in the Peloponnesus declined. By 600 BCE, Greek colonists had set up enclaves in southern France in Massalia (Marseille) and Agde.

At about this time, Indo-European tribes whom the Greeks called Galatai (Gauls) or Keltoi (Celts) had pressed into France from central Europe. (The city of Paris takes its name from the Celtic Parisii tribe that settled in the area.) The Celts—about six to nine million people living within decentralized tribes—were farmers, metalworkers and miners as well as fighters. They practiced animal husbandry, raising hare, ducks and geese along with pigs and cattle. They worked large tracts of land in common using sophisticated agricultural implements. The tribes were expert cheese- and sausage-makers, whose salted meats and hams were exported as far away as Rome. They were, by contemporary accounts, a rowdy bunch. They enjoyed their liquor, whether it was ale or wine, which they took straight. But for all their carousing and feasting, the Gauls watched their waistlines, measuring themselves frequently with a belt.

By 118 BCE, much of southern France or Gaul had become a Roman colony. Rome had wanted to stop territorial incursions by the Celts. It also required large quantities of wheat to feed its people, including its armies, and looked west for supplies. In 52 BCE, Julius Caesar extended Rome's authority across France when he defeated the Gauls at the battle of Alésia, in what is now Burgundy. His victory, one of the major turning points in France's history, made the land a Roman province protected from invasions by Germanic tribes to the north and east. Stability and prosperity helped lay the foundations of modern French culture—a language, a network of roads (some still in use today) for both military and trade purposes, architecture from villas to viaducts, and the art of growing grapes and producing wine.

With Roman domination came shifts in food, diet and dining customs. Wealthy Gallo-Romans built villas that followed the Roman style, including a courtyard or dining room where guests at a dinner party (convivium) would recline instead of sit. At these parties diners would be treated to as many as seven courses, beginning with vegetables, fish or

First century BCE Italian amphora unearthed in the 1990s at Bibracte, a fortified city (*oppidum*) in ancient Gaul, now the site of research and education on Gallic history. Musée de Bibracte. Reprinted with permission.

eggs, followed by meats and poultry, concluding with nuts, fruit and dessert. Foods took on strong flavors, which the Romans preferred, possibly because they suffered from lead poisoning as a result of their use of lead pots. Symptoms included a metallic taste in the mouth, which strong-tasting foods might cover. A more likely reason for the Romans' predilection for pungency was their interest in theories of dietetics. The Romans believed that foods cooked in a certain way could be pathways to better health.

One of the most common flavorings was *garum* or *liquamen,* a fermented fish sauce. It was a staple, factory-produced across the Roman Empire, including Antipolis, what is today the southern French town of Antibes. The Romans also loved a wide variety of spices, but most especially pepper. One of the earliest known cookbooks, *De re coquinaria,* credited to a 1st-century Roman food-lover named Apicius, features recipes almost always including pepper. It was so prized that Germanic tribes demanded 3,000 pounds of pepper as tribute when they stormed Rome's gates in the 5th century.

Invaders from the East

As Rome's influence across Gaul weakened in the 5th and 6th centuries, Visigoths and Franks streamed into France, driven by population pressures and the need for new grazing land. They were, by and large, frugal people, farmers and herders with simple tastes not unlike those of the Celts. Their appetites leaned toward milk, cheese and meats, which were cooked as roasts or stews thickened with barley and oats. They drank hard apple cider and ale, similar to beer but made of fermented grain.

Christianity, which had become the official religion of the Roman Empire early in the 4th century, expanded rapidly into Roman Gaul, and the influence of the Church as a great landowner spread across France. Bread and wine took on symbolic importance, representing in transubstantiation the body and blood of Christ. Christian ritual was grafted onto and subsequently supplanted pagan ritual, extending the power of the Church. With the growth of monasteries and nunneries, the Church took on a significant charitable role, offering hospitality to travelers (with wine from their own vines) and sustenance to the poor. The Church also preserved and passed on the ancient literature on plants, spices, diet and medicine.

But how was a monk to live? While some monastic orders were strict, emphasizing asceticism and abstemiousness as a monk's pathway to heaven, others were not against promoting God's earthly delights, indulging in gustatory pleasures, sometimes to excess. Monasteries were not above showing off their wealth and often hosted fabulous feasts. Indeed, bishops and high clergy, abbots and abbesses were almost always from noble families themselves and ready to entertain benefactors, family and other guests. The opposing traditions of feasting and fasting would reflect the contradictions of Gallo-Christian religious life.

The Middle Ages

Rank and status, not country, defined medieval cuisine, which was more pan-European or international than French. Not surprisingly, the rich ate better than the poor, although preparation methods were fairly uniform, roasting and boiling, salting, smoking and pickling. Meats were cooked in an earthenware pot or iron cauldron called a *chaudière*, hence the English word "chowder." The elites could afford to pay higher prices for provisions, particularly when supply routes were disrupted or products became scarce. For the lowly, rations of typically dark bread made from rye and barley mixed with pea or bean flour were standard, supplemented with gruel or porridge, soup and dairy products.

Peasant life was marked by the seasons, by periods of plenty and insufficiency, even acute hunger and malnutrition, and by the requirements of the Christian calendar, its days of fasting and even abstinence. In spring, summer and fall, food would be abundant, provided there were no crop failures; in winter months it was scarce. Most livestock was slaughtered at the end of the harvest season to spare the cost of over-wintering the animals. Sheep were of particular value for their meat, milk and wool. Meats were salted or smoked; fats rendered and preserved in crocks; herbs dried; fruits, nuts and root crops stored using methods that endured to the 18th century.

But there were also seeds of change. A new ox-drawn plow, invented by Slavs in the 6th century, dramatically increased the amount of land that could be cultivated in the heavy soils of northern Europe. A three-field rotation improved not just the quantity but the quality of a farmer's food, and led to dramatic population growth.

The royal court and its lavish feasts continued to set the tone for fine dining. According to historian Barbara Wheaton, these extraordinary events were primarily "the realizations of aesthetic and social ideals." The festivities, as described by those fortunate enough to be invited, were noteworthy not for individual dishes or particular tastes but for spectacle. Amazing shows underscored the host's wealth and power, a parade of high fashion, food, music and dance. Olivier de la Marche, who helped plan one of the 15th century's most famous parties, the Feast of the Pheasant in 1453, is recorded as saying that the food (he didn't mention the menu) was "rich and copious," "very richly served." It was probably an understatement. This was a time when roasted peacocks were presented in their plumage and blackbirds emerged from baked pies.

At these celebrations, guests were welcomed into the banqueting hall and served at trestle tables topped with white damask tablecloths. A high table on a raised dais dominated the arrangement, and all were seated according to their station, either in a chair or on a common bench. The table settings were minimal compared to today's—a knife and spoon, goblet and tankard. Forks were not yet fashionable. A bread trencher, a sturdy slice of stale whole-wheat bread baked several days ahead, would hold a serving of sliced meat. Special guests received the best pieces of meat and additional trenchers. At truly luxurious banquets, diners were treated to silver or gold plates. King François I ordered the first plates in 1536 and his grandson Henri III is credited with

Detail from the 11th century Bayeux Tapestry, the medieval masterpiece that recounts William the Conqueror's victory over the English at Hastings in 1066. Preparations are being made for an open-air feast—chickens roasted on skewers, stews cooked over an open fire.

introducing the use of forks. Pages circulating among the guests would serve wine diluted with water, a stronger drink considered bad form.

Wheaton says a dinner menu might be made up of three courses, with multiple dishes for each. The first course might include fish-liver turnovers, a meat stew with cinnamon sauce, ox-marrow fritters, eel stew, freshwater fish in broth with a green sage sauce, more meat, more fish. For the second course, there was a roast, meat larded and boiled, or spiced, chopped and topped with crayfish tails, capon pasties, crisp pancakes, eels, more fish and blancmange. This thick, sweet dish was made from white or light-colored meat such as veal or chicken breast, cooked in almond milk or water, shredded and combined with powdered nuts, sugar, breadcrumbs or rice. Finally, diners could sup on frumenty (wheat berries boiled in broth, a typical accompaniment to venison), lamprey in a hot sauce, fish and turnovers. Dessert would be a spiced wine called hippocras, wafers, raisins, nuts and fruit.

Spices and strong sauces popular among the Gallo-Romans continued to be hallmarks of medieval cookery. A medieval chef such as the famous Guillaume Tirel or Taillevent, who served three French kings and is credited with writing *Le Viandier*, one of the earliest cookbooks, was likely to use liberal amounts of vinegar or verjuice (from sour grapes) in his dishes, to mix

William and his nobles are served at a banquet table, while Odo, Bishop of Bayeux, gives the blessing. The tapestry documents culinary implements as well as a wide variety of meats served, washed down with wine. By special permission of the City of Bayeux.

fruits with meat to create sweet and sour, even bitter, tastes. Although some herbs and spices, such as ginger, mustard, caraway, cardamom, coriander and cumin, could be grown in a kitchen garden (*potager*), others, such as pepper, cinnamon, nutmeg, mace and cloves, had to be imported from the east. Spices were not used to camouflage the taste of rotting meat. Smoking and salting were more reliable methods for curing. Besides, if you could afford spices, you probably could also command a reliable cut.

Sweets and confections, too, were fashionable. Cane sugar made its way into the European diet as contact between Islamic and western cultures increased. After the Crusades and with calmer cultural exchanges, exotic fruits such as oranges, bananas, lemons and dates were brought to France.

Toward a New World

While the medieval style of cooking, with its emphasis on spicy, sweet and sour sauces, continued into the Renaissance, new foods became available during the exploration and mapping of the Americas, resulting in the importation of dozens of strange animal and plant species. Not all of these foods found ready acceptance. Tomatoes were thought to be poisonous, potatoes to cause leprosy. It would take two hundred years for the potato to make its way into French stews and soups. But other foods, such as strawberries, pineapple, guava, yams, beans, bell peppers, pumpkin and maize, were readily incorporated into the French diet, largely because they fit in with existing tastes. The turkey, or *poulet d'Inde* (later shortened to *dinde*), found favor because it was bigger, meatier and moister than popular domestic fowl and game birds.

The number of different vegetables cultivated in French kitchen and botanical gardens increased severalfold. A 14th-century manuscript on household management, *Le Ménagier de Paris*, lists over a dozen varieties grown by its author: carrots, chard, cress, fava beans, leeks, lettuce, onions, parsley, peas, spinach, fennel and turnips. By the 17th century, another writer, Nicholas de Bonnefons, a political and social climber attached to the royal household, would recommend more, including black salsify, broccoli, celery, kohlrabi and lentils. Vegetables were taking on a vital place in the French diet.

The food divide between rich and poor, however, scarcely improved and may even have gotten worse. Unable to afford exotic imports or risk experimenting with new cultivars, the peasantry and working classes had to make do with the old standbys—leeks and garlic, peas and beans, turnips and cabbage, and dark bread. And there was less consumption of meat. France's population, reduced by 50 percent in successive outbreaks of bubonic plague during the 14th and early 15th centuries, now had recovered sufficiently to put pressure on existing meat and grain supplies. The poor could no longer afford them. The Hundred Years War, followed by the 16th century's Wars of Religions, added to the general misery, severely disturbing agrarian life and aggravating food shortages. In the early 1600s, King Henry IV's wish that his subjects enjoy a weekly *poule au pot*—the equivalent of a chicken in every pot—was a faint hope for most.

Coming of Age

If 17th-century French cooking had been a fusion of spicy, sweet and sour, by the beginning of the 18th century everything would be turned on its edge. Instead of clobbering meats and vegetables, disguising texture and flavor, cooks would seize on a radical approach—to keep things simple, to bring out a food's natural tastes.

The man most associated with this taste revolution was François Pierre, also known as La Varenne, in charge of the household of the Marquis d'Uxelles. (The well-known dish of mushrooms sautéed with herbs and shallots is named after him.) Although La Varenne didn't claim credit for the new style of cooking, he codified it in two cookbooks intended for culinary professionals, *Le Cuisinier françois*, first published in 1651, and *Le Pâtissier françois*, in 1653. In these books, La Varenne laid the foundations for a classical cuisine devoted to balance and harmony. He advocated roasting the best cuts of meat and stewing the rest; reducing liquids to concentrate their flavor; mixing flour and fat into a roux then adding liquids such as bouillon or cream to create sauces; and using herbs tied in a bouquet garni to flavor stocks. Another culinary trendsetter, Nicolas de Bonnefons, whose *Délices de la campagne* was published at about the same time as La Varenne's cookbooks, also espoused this style of delicate cooking but, significantly, addressed his remarks to the heads of bourgeois households instead of the pros.

Other factors encouraged this more natural cuisine. As spices became available without difficulty, they were no longer viewed as luxuries and went out of fashion. Fruits and vegetables were now more exciting and exclusive, especially when brought to market at their peak of freshness and fragility.

Enlightenment thinking and neoclassical style would also tout the virtues of a simple and virtuous life. François Menon, writing in 1742, would coin the term *"nouvelle cuisine"* and acknowledge in the title of his cookbook, *La Cuisinière bourgeoise,* that in all but the wealthiest households, French women were the chief cooks. A new, waist-high brick and tile stove was enabling cooks to move away from the open hearth and facilitating food preparation that required attention to detail.

Among the tastemakers, Louis XIV (1638–1715) had been a conservative holdout. The Sun King had preferred his food the old-fashioned way— spiced. Louis loved eating, and he had prodigious tastes, using his fingers at the royal dinner table instead of a fork. His favorite drinking water was shipped from central France to his chateau at Versailles. But he encouraged his gardener, Jean-Baptiste de la Quintinie, to cultivate exotic fruits in glass houses called *orangeries.*

Although the court still played a significant part in promoting mode and manners, it was an emerging upper middle class, particularly in Paris, that was truly shaping taste. By the mid-17th century, Paris was in the midst of a building boom, its population having exploded to a million people. Parisians needed provisioning on a large scale and wealthy inhabitants had the money to command special goods. Specialty and neighborhood markets grew up around the city. The city's historic central market, Les Halles, established in

From the 1693 English edition of Jean-Baptiste de la Quintinie's *The Compleat Gard'ner.* As Louis XIV's royal gardener, de la Quintinie implemented a variety of innovations at Versailles, including planting exotic vegetables and fruit trees. Courtesy of the Department of Special Collections, Memorial Library, University of Wisconsin–Madison.

the 12th century, was both an important wholesale and retail emporium. (It was demolished in 1971 and moved to Rungis, south of Paris.) Culinary professionals from various guilds—bakers (*boulangers*), butchers (*charcutiers*), caterers (*traiteurs*) and spice merchants (*épiciers*)—were hard at work.

The up-to-the-minute drink was chocolate, especially at breakfast instead of the usual soup or porridge. A New World food, cocoa had crossed the Atlantic from Mexico to Spain, where it became fashionable at court. Coffee, too, was an exotic drink, believed to have medicinal properties. Originally from Ethiopia and the Arab world, it had traveled to Turkey and across the Mediterranean to Marseille. The Turkish ambassador to France had also introduced the drink at Versailles in 1669. Soon, *cafés* spread across Paris, the first one a stall set up by an Armenian merchant. Francesco-Procopio dei Coltelli followed suit, starting a chain of shops, among them the Left Bank's enduring Le Procope. The *café* became a new public sphere for intellectual discussion, even revolutionary thought.

By the 1760s, a new eatery began to flourish, serving hearty and healthfully restorative meat or poultry broths called *restaurants*. Other light foods such as rice pudding and soft-boiled eggs were also served. By the end of the 18th century, a *restaurant* referred to the establishment, not just the dish. Unlike

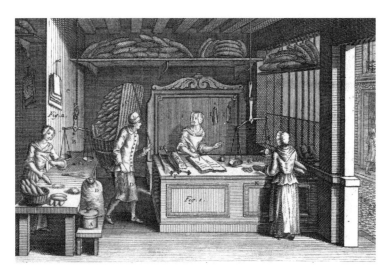

The baker's art, from workroom to salesroom, is detailed in J.E. Bertrand's *Descriptions des arts et métiers*, Neuchatel, Imprimerie de la Société Typographique, 1771–83. Courtesy of the Department of Special Collections, Memorial Library, University of Wisconsin–Madison.

tables d'hôte, where diners ate family-style, these new venues seated customers at individual tables. Dining could be more refined and intimate.

Virtually all of these advances had little place in the life of the rural poor, whose condition remained precarious. Most families could not raise enough crops and livestock for food, and relied on bread for 95 percent of their calories. Beyond war and disease, a series of famines in the late 17th and 18th centuries was disastrous, a sobering contrast to the excesses of, by then, a nearly bankrupt French court.

Beyond Revolution

By the end of the 18th century French cuisine represented simplicity, naturalness, authenticity and healthful eating, but there still were moments when kitchens produced creations that were over the top. It is not surprising then that, after the French Revolution in 1789 and the ensuing Reign of Terror (1793–1794), lavish dining came back into vogue. With increasing frequency, food in fancy restaurants and upper-class households was served in the Russian not French style. For centuries, *service à la française*—multiple dishes brought to the table at one time, and usually lukewarm after a long trip from the kitchen—had characterized French dining. The fashion reached its height during the reign of Louis XIV. By contrast, *service à la russe*, so-called because Russia's ambassador introduced it in 1810, emphasized a few dishes served sequentially and, more typically, hot.

One of the great pacesetters was Charles-Maurice de Talleyrand-Périgord, diplomat and political survivor par excellence. Beyond his consummate bargaining skills, he was a gourmet and a wine connoisseur. In 1797, he hired Antonin Carême as his pastry chef. Carême, who later went on to work for Alexander I of Russia and the Rothschild banking family, has been called the greatest cook of all time, the King of Chefs and Chef of Kings. He authored several cookbooks that organized French cuisine in ways that are still honored today. He adapted a cuisine associated with the aristocracy to more middle-class audiences, but still laid out plans for opulent dining, including the construction of extravagant food centerpieces or *pièces montées*.

Restaurants, which had flourished in the 18th century, now exploded, their numbers jumping from about 100 establishments in the 1780s to about 3,000 in just 40 years. Although some were still modest eateries, much like their predecessors, others were among the first gastronomic restaurants extending luxurious dining to those who could afford it. At the Café des Anglais, head chef Adolphe Dugléré, Carême's protegé, named dishes after his high-society clientele—*pommes Anna* (thinly sliced potatoes cooked in butter) for a famous actress or courtesan and *potage Germiny* (sorrel soup) after the governor of the Bank of France. The menu at Les Trois Frères, operated by three brothers from Provence, featured regional dishes such as *bouillabaisse* (fish soup) and *brandade de morue* (creamed salt cod).

After the French Revolution, France was recast politically into administrative units or departments in an effort to create a more unified nation. In 1804, Napoleon's new civil code, which revolutionized French government, instituted the metric system and regularized weights and measures. (Napoleon can also be credited with promoting the cultivation of sugar beets after British sailors blocked delivery of colonial sugar cane to French ports.) Shortly thereafter, Alexandre Balthazar Laurent Grimod de la Reynière announced his own code, one for food lovers, in his *Almanach des gourmands*. Grimod was an aristocrat, trained as a lawyer, but probably best known for being the first of a new breed of food philosopher–critics. In his writings he recommended culinary simplicity and set down a system of taste-testing for judging excellence. Jean-Anthelme Brillat-Savarin was another epicure. His *Physiologie du goût* ("physiology of taste"), published in 1825, has been called the most celebrated treatise on gastronomy ever written. "Tell me what you eat," Brillat-Savarin said, "and I will tell you what you are." Dining now could be a cultural activity on a par with enjoying music and art.

Scientific and technical advances also affected French cooking. New developments in transportation made it easier to distribute foodstuffs around the country. Food sterilization and packaging in jars and cans, pasteurization and commercial refrigeration would affect eating patterns, too. With the advent of gas lamps and electricity, restaurants could keep longer hours. What remained constant was the commitment to the supremacy of fresh ingredients and preparations that honored natural goodness and taste.

By the turn of the 19th century, a mostly urban restaurant culture was flourishing. Master cooks such as Auguste Escoffier were dazzling well-heeled patrons. Escoffier brought new attention to the basics surrounding preparation of sauces, stocks and pastries. He laid down rules for menu composition, stipulating distinct courses, such as fish and meat. He insisted on contrasting tastes and textures. For instance, a crunchy cookie or biscuit needed to accompany a creamy dessert. Escoffier also reorganized the professional kitchen into stations—positions of responsibility, such as the

The pleasures of spit-roasted chicken are suggested in a 1915 English edition of Jean-Anthelme Brillat-Savarin's *Physiologie du goût*, entitled *A Handbook of Gastronomy*. Courtesy of the Department of Special Collections, Memorial Library, University of Wisconsin–Madison.

garde-manger for cold dishes and the *saucier* for sauces. The system remains in place today. More-affordable shops with fixed-price menus were also spreading, patronized by the middle and working classes. Whatever one's fortunes, a public eating culture was on the rise across society.

Modern Times

Sumptuous meals once enjoyed by the upper classes could no longer be justified after the devastating effects of World War I. Cooking became simpler, even "democratic," with the emphasis on nutrition, the accent placed squarely on eating more vegetables and less meat. Even before the war, regional dishes had become fashionable and been incorporated into haute cuisine menus. Now these local traditional foods were given the spotlight instead of the elaborate creations associated with high-society chefs.

France was predominantly an agricultural country, with two thirds of the population living in rural areas at the turn of the 20th century. Despite technological innovation, French farming practices had remained traditional, even "pre-industrial." Households struggled to be self-sufficient, producing most of a family's food. The mainstay of the rural diet was still soup, arguably then and now the fundamental French dish. Germany's occupation of France during World War II presented other hardships for the populace. Some of France's best meat and dairy products were diverted to the German Reich, rationing limited food intake to 1,300 calories and life expectancy plummeted.

Between the wars, with the rise of the automobile and better roads, a gastronomic tourism had taken hold. The French could go "on the road" in search of fine food. One of the 20th century's most celebrated connoisseurs, Maurice Sailland or "Curnonsky," provided directions by way of his writings, promoting local restaurants and regional wines and dishes. The first Michelin Guide, produced by the French tire company for drivers and cyclists, was published in 1900. Its one-star rating signifying good food was implemented in 1926, the three-star system in 1931. Among the first to receive top honors was Fernand Point's La Pyramide, in Vienne, south of Lyon. Today, Michelin ratings continue to be hotly sought after, contested and even ignored.

Concerns about food production, food purity and safety encouraged new government regulations, including a certification system, called *appellation d'origine contrôlée* in 1935. The A.O.C. built upon a protective measure that was established in 1855 by Bordeaux winegrowers and recognized a special connection between place and taste—where particular grapes were grown and how the wines were produced. The government's A.O.C. legislation extended protections beyond Bordeaux. Other agricultural products, especially cheese, would be included after 1990, with the A.O.C. designation conferring an honored pedigree, a label that evoked *terroir*.

Travel across France today and you will regularly come across *terroir* in phrases like *menu de terroir* or *goût de terroir*. The word is difficult to translate—it means more than the land or soil, territory or climate, even the way farmers till their fields. Despite the marketing hyperbole often associated with the term, *terroir* evokes food memories, feelings of belonging and connection, tradition, nostalgia and, more fundamentally, pleasure. It is an idea firmly rooted in assumptions about French history and culture, a conviction that foods will taste different based on their origin.

Postmodern France: Is French Food Dead?

In the postwar period, the French could celebrate their country's culinary riches again. Meat returned to the French diet as a mainstay, and white bread became preferred over the war's coarser, browner stuff. Restaurant owner–managers formed their own association of master chefs in 1951, the

Association des Maîtres Cuisiniers, promoting gastronomic eateries run by a breed of independent cooks not afraid to experiment, people like Paul Bocuse, Jean Troigros, Pierre Troigros, Roger Vergé and Michel Guérard.

To these rising stars (and eventually superstars), freshness was paramount. They cultivated relationships with local producers to ensure their restaurants got the best ingredients. In the kitchen, they concocted fruit and vegetable reductions, preferring them to heavier, classical sauces based on butter and flour. Plating dishes, a *service à l'assiette,* was favored over tableside service *en salle,* so that the chef could have complete control over a meal. They were not against reintroducing spices, acknowledging foreign flavors and mixing up different kinds of food, such as foie gras with lobster. Guidebook authors Henri Gault and Christian Millau called this gastronomic campaign against conservative cooking *"nouvelle cuisine,"* coining again the term François Menon had used two centuries earlier. It was a culinary avant-garde that in its own way mirrored political and social upheavals in France in the 1960s.

Since then, some have argued that not just haute cuisine but French food generally has gone sharply downhill. In his captivating book, *Au Revoir To All That,* journalist Michael Steinberger has stated that French cooking is now in crisis, with few encouraging signs. He lists a host of reasons— misguided politics that created rigid employment regulations and economic stagnation; less-than-rigorous professional training that tested prospective chefs not on foundational cooking but on how to use a variety of processed and prepared foods; and with more French women in the workforce, less cooking at home. Steinberger states that by 2008 France had 40,000 cafés, down from 200,000 in the 1960s, while McDonald's could boast it was the country's largest private-sector employer, with more than 1,000 fast-food outlets. Steinberger also discounts France's Slow Food movement, which has a significantly smaller membership than Italy and the US.

And yet, Steinberger sees reason for hope. Another generation of committed but also economy-minded chefs is pioneering again, creating in something called *bistronomie* a movement that is breaking the rules, playing with ingredients, having fun with flavors, while staying true to good food.

If there's any doubt whether French food is alive and kicking, all one has to do is observe the French at table. Taste matters to the French; they savor what they are eating, and they take their time about it. The French have resisted the introduction of genetically modified foods; across the European Union, it is illegal to sell as food animals treated with growth hormones.

Fernand Point (with bow tie), his wife Mado and the kitchen crew of La Pyramide, Point's celebrated restaurant in Vienne, among the first to be awarded Michelin's three stars in 1933. A young disciple, Paul Bocuse, is to Point's right. Reprinted with permission of Paul Bocuse.

French sociologist Claude Fischler, in a far-reaching comparative study, has analyzed what sets the French apart, particularly from Americans. His research shows that although both French and Americans are equally concerned about making healthy food choices, more French people see themselves as healthy eaters than do Americans. Yet they don't obsess over what they consume, don't feel as guilty over occasional treats, and still are, despite increasing rates of obesity, among the leanest people in the developing world. For the French, eating is synonymous with pleasure and dining is a communal experience. Alas, for Americans, so absorbed with low-fat food, fad diets and caloric intake, it seems quite the reverse.

Ultimately, what may define French cooking is not France's varied climate and diversified environments, or its claims to regional cuisines, even its reputation as the country that invented haute cuisine. In the end, French cooking may be defined by a heightened sense of aesthetics, a commitment to pleasure and a devotion to sociability. It is an obsession about food as well as a point of national pride.

REGIONS

1. **The North and Northeast:** Nord-Pas-de-Calais, Picardy, Champagne, Lorraine and Alsace
2. **The East:** Franche-Comté, Rhône-Alps and Burgundy
3. **The South:** Provence-Alps-Côte-d'Azur and the Languedoc-Roussillon
4. **The Southwest:** Midi-Pyrenees and Aquitaine
5. **The West:** Poitou-Charentes, Brittany, Normandy and Pays de la Loire
6. **The Heartland:** Limousin, Auvergne and Val-de-Loire
7. **The Île-de-France:** Paris and suburbs

Regional French Food

A Quick Tour of French Foods and Their Regional Variations

French Food in a Nutshell

The French diet is extremely varied, based on a wide assortment of meat, game, fish and poultry, fruits, vegetables, starches and dairy products, as well as other foodstuffs. At the heart of French food is the trinity of bread (*pain*), wine (*vin*) and cheese (*fromage*).

It has become a cliché, shorthand for French culture, the image of a Frenchman sporting a beret and carrying a baguette, that two-foot long crusty wand. Beginning in the 18th century, certain refinements—a new method to remove bran, the development of yeast and the advent of kneading machines—made it possible to bake loaves of white bread. At first reserved for the nobility, these loaves began to make an appearance around Paris. In Revolutionary, egalitarian France, what was good for Parisians was deemed equally so for the country folk. Still, it was not until the 20th century that the dark, round, whole-meal loaf once associated with the peasantry was displaced by the baguette.

Bread, whatever its shape, has been at the center of French culture for centuries. It has been the staff of life, the mainstay of the French diet, a significant portion of caloric intake, especially among the poor. At almost every juncture in French history, bread has been a major player. From a Christian point of view, bread along with wine symbolized one of the Church's most powerful rituals, Holy Communion. With the fear of famine all too real and the search for food a constant preoccupation, bread served as nothing less than the guarantor of social stability and, as such, received subsidies from the state. Government regulations could specify bread's content, its size and price.

Although diets are now much more diversified, with bread consumption around 150 grams daily (the equivalent of a few slices) compared to about 900 grams in the 18th century, no meal is complete without bread.

Beginning in the late 1950s, the quality of bread began to decline with the introduction of a more mechanized manufacturing process and a variety of time- and labor-saving techniques. Increasingly, bakers seeded their dough with industrial yeast and relied on additives to give the bread elasticity. Gone was the tradition of more-natural sourdough fermentations based on a starter culture, and along with it both a level of skill and actual taste. But with increased interest in nutrition and concern over the loss of the baguette's flavor, a new generation of bakers emerged to lead a bread revival that re-emphasized artisanal baking. One of the leaders of this return to basics was Lionel Poilâne, "the most prestigious baker of his time," according to historian Steven Kaplan. Kaplan asserts that a loaf labeled *pain de tradition* must be made without additives. *Pain de maison* must be produced from start to finish on the premises. He advises people to judge bread based on appearance, crust, crumb (the soft inner portion), odor and aroma, taste, flavor and harmony. The crumb should be off-white, springy, moist and with definite cavities or "eyes."

French bread is usually cut at the last moment, just before a meal. Bread is rarely served with butter, except at breakfast, and sits directly on the table or tablecloth, rather than on a side plate. Bread is eaten throughout a meal, in small mouthfuls, and can serve as a tool to collect sauce from a plate or help place a piece of salad on a fork. Although sandwiches are popular, these are usually for picnics or meals on the go.

Poilâne bread, made from stone-ground flour, sourdough starter, water and salt, and baked in wood-fired ovens, recalls a more traditional loaf than the baguette.

To the French, wine adds an essential element to the taste of a dish and therefore to its appreciation. Much care and attention is paid to pairing particular wines and foods. Wine is also used extensively in cooking to tenderize or add flavor to foods. However, government efforts to promote health and reduce alcohol-related highway fatalities seem to have succeeded. Although it is not uncommon for two people to finish a bottle of wine together over a meal, the French, on average, drink about a glass of wine per day—some two-thirds less than they did in the 1930s.

Still, France is one of the world's largest wine producers, with a tradition of wine production dating back two thousand years to Greek and Roman colonists. Wine culture spread across the land in the Middle Ages thanks largely to the Church, which used wine in the Catholic Mass as well as secular celebrations. Today, wine grapes are grown in almost every region of the country, with the possible exception of the Northwest.

Historically, Champagne, Burgundy and Bordeaux have been acknowledged as the great wine-producing centers, followed by the Rhône and Loire valleys. But top-quality vintages have also emerged from the Languedoc-Roussillon region in southern France and from Alsace in the northeast. A wine's character will depend on the particular type of grape, where it is grown (its *terroir* or, as wine writer Andrew Jefford puts it, its "placeness"), the weather in a given year and the production methods that are used.

Rules are not hard and fast concerning when to drink red, white or rosé wines. Champagne may be dry (*brut*) or sweet (*sec* and *demi-sec*). Some white and red wines may be light and fruity, others full-bodied and complex. As a general rule, Bordeaux reds are made from Cabernet, Cabernet Franc and Merlot grapes, Burgundy reds from Pinot Noir, and Beaujolais from Gamay. Burgundy whites are produced from Chardonnay grapes. For Rhône Valley reds, the building blocks are Grenache, Syrah and Viognier. Alsace and the Loire Valley are esteemed for their white wines. Gewürztraminer, Pinot Blanc, Pinot Gris and Riesling are the Alsatian varietals; Sauvignon, Chenin Blanc and Muscadet are those for the Loire. The Loire's reds, from Cabernet Franc and Pinot Noir grapes, are also highly touted. Readers interested in more specific information are encouraged to consult wine guides.

While wine is central to a meal, aperitifs and liqueurs play a vital role before and after dinner. For centuries, the production of liqueurs was associated with monasteries and pharmacies. Two famous examples are

Benedictine, distilled along the Normandy coast, and Chartreuse, made in the eastern Chartreuse Mountains, although the liqueur is no longer manufactured at the monastery but in a factory in the nearby town of Voiron. Dutch traders may take credit for giving a boost to the production of French spirits. In the 18th century, the Dutch, who had a foothold around the Atlantic town of Cognac, realized that it would be far more economical to distill their brandy on the premises than to ship it to distillers back home. Cognac, made from grapes, is distilled twice and aged in oak casks for several years, depending on the grade. Armagnac, produced around Bordeaux, is a single-distillation aged brandy with an earthier taste. Calvados is a single-distillation aged apple brandy from Normandy. Pastis is a popular anise-flavored aperitif, similar to Greece's ouzo. Transparent when undiluted, it characteristically turns milky with the usual addition of water. While pastis may have a stronger following in the south of France, it is drunk around the country and may owe its popularity to the prohibition of absinthe in the early 1900s. Absinthe once was feared as highly addictive, but its psychoactive properties may have been exaggerated.

Charles de Gaulle once lectured that you could not easily bring a country together when it had 250 different kinds of cheese. The exact number today may be subject to debate—some argue more, others less. But there is no disputing that France is a cheese-lover's paradise. Cheese is usually served as a separate course at both lunch and dinner, just before and sometimes in place of dessert. A server may present a selection of cheeses on a platter or trolley. The diner is expected to indicate which varieties are of most interest so that the server can cut wedges (usually three) and transfer them onto a small plate. Local restaurants often showcase local cheeses. When sampling several cheeses, it is a good idea to begin with the mildest before moving on to more robust ones. Other good sources for local cheeses are farmers' markets and cheese shops (*fromageries*), where the staff may have special expertise in *affinage,* the storing and aging of cheese.

Cheeses are classified by milk source—cow (*vache*), ewe (*brebis*) or goat (*chèvre*)—and by the particular methods of production. Cheeses may be either farmhouse (*fermier*), artisanal or industrial (*industriel*). They may be manufactured from pasteurized or raw milk (*lait cru*), and aged from several days to a few months. Cheeses come in different shapes and sizes and range in their butterfat content (*matière grasse*). Most French cheeses are about 45–50% butterfat, but *triple-crème* cheeses such as Brillat-Savarin are 75% butterfat. At the other extreme is Tomme de Savoie, which is sometimes made from skim milk, but nevertheless full-flavored and complex.

Here are a few categories that may be useful in identifying cheeses. *Fromages à croûte fleurie,* or "blooming" cheeses, are soft in texture, typically are made from cow's milk and feature a velvety white mold. Examples are Normandy's famed Camembert (most are now mass-produced and less than 10% are made from raw milk) and Neufchâtel, a heart-shaped cheese dating back to the 11th century. *Fromages à croûte lavée* are washed-rind cheeses. The washing process involves immersion in liquids such as brine, wine or spirits. The washing slows the growth of bloom, but promotes the development of bacteria and along with them interesting smells and tastes. Examples of these soft, cow's-milk cheeses are Époisses, a specialty of Burgundy, and the square-shaped Maroilles or Marolle. *Fromages à pâte persillée* are blue-veined cheeses such as ewe's-milk Roquefort, which benefited from royal protection beginning in the 15th century. *Fromages à pâte pressée* are pressed cheeses that may be medium-firm or hard. Morbier has a characteristic midline of ash, which today is more typically an edible vegetable product added to simulate the traditional layer of ash. Other pressed cheeses available across France are Cantal and Comté. Among the more popular *fromages de chèvre,* or goat's-milk cheeses, are Banon, a Provençal cheese traditionally wrapped in chestnut leaves, and Crottin de Chavignol, an earthy-tasting disk-shaped cheese from the Loire. More than three dozen cheeses have A.O.C. status.

There is a misconception that the French do not like milk (*lait*). France is a dairy nation and dairy products (beyond butter and cheese) play a significant role in the diet. Children drink milk either plain or mixed in hot chocolate, which is usually served in a large cup or bowl (*bol*). Adults sip milk in their morning *cafés au lait* or *crèmes*. Milk and cream are used in

In a nation that boasts hundreds of cheeses, Neufchâtel, a heart-shaped cow's-milk cheese, can claim to date back to the 11th century.

soups and sauces. *Crème fraîche,* which resembles sour cream but has a higher fat content and special pungency from lactic acid fermentation, is often used as a thickener with stews. Yogurt, which became popular in France in the 1960s, is commonly eaten at breakfast or served at lunch and dinner instead of a cheese course or dessert. *Fromage blanc* (also called *fromage frais*), made from curdled cow's milk, is similar to a whipped cottage cheese. It is also widely consumed either plain, with herbs, or sweetened with sugar, honey or jam. A richer version of *fromage blanc* is *faisselle,* so-called because it is sold in a small plastic strainer, which permits the whey to drain away.

The French are big meat (*viande*) eaters, outdone only, per capita, by Australians and Americans. That makes them major producers and major importers of beef (*bœuf*) and poultry (*volaille*). But the French are not beef-centric, enjoying lamb (*agneau*), pork (*porc*), veal (*veau*), goat (*chèvre*), venison (*venaison, chevreuil*) and wild or farm-raised boar (*sanglier, marcassin*). French beef is not as marbled as in the US, and cuts are typically smaller and more varied. Beef stew is a general menu item but its ingredients will vary with the recipe and region. The French prefer their meat served rare and it is advisable to specify how you want yours cooked (*cuisson*) to avoid any surprises. (See *bœuf,* p. 108.)

The French consume most parts of the animal, from feet to snout, and are likely to appreciate organ meat. Frequently seen on menus are veal sweetbreads (*ris de veau*), calf kidneys (*rognons de veau*) and beef stomach (*tripe à la mode de Caen*). There is a long tradition of smoking and curing meats in France. Sausage could be stored for months, an important

French breakfasts often begin with a bowl (*bol*) of steaming hot chocolate (*chocolat chaud*) or *café au lait,* enjoyed with French bread, butter and jam (*tartine*), which is more usual fare than a croissant.

advantage well into the mid-20th century when refrigerators were still uncommon across much of France. Although sausage is readily available today at supermarkets, markets, delicatessens and butcher shops, French hosts may still take satisfaction in being able to offer guests homemade varieties studded with special ingredients such as pistachios and truffles, particular herbs and spices, and wine or spirits. Sausage is eaten hot or cold, in a sandwich, as an appetizer or main course. *Saucisse* needs to be cooked; *saucisson* is cured or smoked. Familiar types are blood sausage made from pork (*boudin noir*), which is first poached and then pan-fried; chitterling sausage (*andouille* and *andouillette*) made from pork intestines; pork sausage spread (*rillettes*); and a North African lamb or beef sausage (*merguez*), spiced with a chile paste (*harissa*) and fennel seeds. There are regional sausage varieties, with Lyon historically a respected center for sausage making (*charcuterie*).

Eating horsemeat was proscribed by the Church during the Middle Ages but in the 19th century was promoted by the government as an inexpensive alternative to eating beef. Today, horsemeat is still sold in special butcher shops (*boucheries chevalines*) but is mostly imported from central Europe and North America. It may be enjoying something of a comeback as an inexpensive and exotic meat.

Several different kinds of poultry are available, such as chicken (*poulet*), duck (*canard*), goose (*oie*), guinea hen (*pintade*) and turkey (*dinde*), as well as partridge (*perdreau*), pheasant (*faisan*), quail (*caille*) and woodcock (*bécasse*). The French make significant cooking distinctions depending on the age or sex of the bird. A tender *poulet* or *poularde,* a specially fattened young chicken, will be deemed suitable for roasting, but a mature hen (*poule*) and capon (*chapon*) typically will be stewed. The A.O.C.-designated *poulet de Bresse* is a specific breed, given a special diet until almost twice the age of usual supermarket chicken. Rabbit (*lapin*), which is widely accepted and sold along with poultry, is available both wild and farm-raised.

Eggs (*œufs*) are a significant source of protein but are rarely seen at the breakfast table. Hard-boiled eggs are on hand at some cafés as snacks, kept on the counter in small metal canisters. More customary egg dishes are omelets, filled with herbs, cheese or ham, served for lunch or a light dinner along with a salad; and poached eggs, a common first course. Eggs are also used extensively in quiches, custard dishes and desserts.

The consumption of foie gras, the fattened liver of ducks and geese, dates back centuries. The Romans force-fed their geese figs. It is possible that in 16th-century France, Jewish families, whose dietary laws encouraged eating poultry over meat, may have helped popularize foie gras. But it wasn't until the 18th century that it became fashionable, baked in a pie with chopped pork. Although the practice of force-feeding birds with grain has been criticized in some quarters, foie gras continues to be enjoyed across France, with production centered in the south and southwest. The livers may also be imported from central Europe and packaged locally. Large sections or lobes of foie gras are usually served sautéed or baked as a first course. Foie gras can also be puréed, and often mixed with other fats, into a pâté, which is typically spread on toast. Duck and goose confits are meats that have been conserved through cooking in their own fat.

France's geography ensures that fish (*poisson*) and shellfish (*coquillages* and *crustacés*) are never far from the dining table. The country is bounded along the west and south by water—the English Channel, Atlantic Ocean and Mediterranean Sea—and the heartland is fed by rivers and streams. But in France, as in many parts of the world, fish stocks are increasingly threatened by over-fishing, pollution and invasive species. Fish and shellfish are often commercially farm-raised and brought to market from a multiplicity of French and global sources. Restaurants routinely include a variety of fish dishes on their menus. Readers are encouraged to ask their server about the provenance of a particular fish or shellfish.

While firm-fleshed fish like bass (*bar, loup de mer*), haddock (*églefin*), salmon (*saumon*), sole (*sole*), trout (*truite*), tuna (*thon*) and turbot (*turbot*) are common to both American and European tables, other types of fish found in France may be unfamiliar to North Americans. One of these is eel, both salt- and freshwater. Another example is monkfish, also called anglerfish (*lotte* or *baudroie*), a firm, chunky fish that tastes a little like lobster and is often grilled or prepared in soups and stews. Its ugly, primeval-looking head makes it easy to identify in shops, provided that it hasn't been cut off. Skate (*raie*) is poached and served with butter and capers. There are many regional variations of fish stew, including Provence's beloved *bouillabaisse*.

While not an exhaustive list, here are some salt- and freshwater fish to look for: pandora or red sea bream (*pageot*), which is often broiled or fried; red mullet (*rouget*); and fresh sardines, usually grilled. Flatfish, such as brill (*barbue*), dab or lemon sole (*limande*) and plaice (*carrelet*), are often poached or sautéed. Cod (*cabillaud* or *morue fraîche*); hake (*colin, lieu noir* or *merlu*); John Dory, which is similar to porgy (*Saint-Pierre*); and whiting (*merlan*) are popular menu items, as are migratory and freshwater fish such as shad (*alose*), smelt (*éperlan*), bream (*brème*), carp (*carpe*), char (*omble*), and pike and perch varieties (*sandre* and *brochet*).

The French consume a wide variety of shellfish, especially oysters (*huîtres*), mostly farm-raised. France is Europe's largest oyster producer, harvesting more than 100,000 tons annually, mostly along the Atlantic coast. Two types of oysters are harvested in France. The *Ostrea edulis* or flat-shelled oyster (*plate*), is native to France, but was virtually wiped out by pollution and disease in the 20th century. The convex-shelled (*creuse*) or Pacific oyster, *Crassostrea gigas,* was then introduced from Japan and Canada, and is now commonly produced. Oysters are identified by their origin. *Bouzigues*, from the Mediterranean, are convex-shelled oysters. *Belons* are flat-shelled oysters raised at the mouth of the Bélon River in Brittany. *Arcachons*, also flat-shelled, are harvested along the south-Atlantic coast around Bordeaux. *Marennes* are convex-shelled oysters raised farther north in the Marennes-Oléron region, France's largest oyster cultivation area. Here oysters are fattened in saltwater ponds (*claires*) and have a marked taste of the sea. They are graded, depending on the amount of time spent in the salt pools, as *claires, fines de claires* and *spéciales de claires. Marennes* may have a blue-green tinge from algae (*navicule bleue*).

Because of oyster farming and easy refrigeration, the old maxim about not eating oysters during months that contain the letter "r"—months when the oysters reproduced—no longer holds. Oysters are graded by size, the lower the number the larger the size. Menus usually indicate how many are in an order. When eaten raw, on the half-shell, oysters are served with lemon juice or a splash of vinegar and shallots along with rye bread and butter. This is one of the rare times the French take their bread with butter. (Be advised that the consumption of raw or undercooked foods may increase the risk of food-borne illness.) Oysters are also cooked in a variety of ways, including poached, fried, baked and stewed.

Other popular kinds of shellfish include mussels (*moules*) and scallops (*coquilles Saint-Jacques*). Smaller varieties, such as cockles (*coques*) and periwinkles (*bigorneaux*), are often included along with oysters, clams (*palourdes* and *praires*), large crabs (*tourteaux*) and lobsters (*homards*) on high, tiered metal platters (*plateaux de fruits de mer*) ordered in restaurants at celebratory meals. Raw shellfish is served cold on ice, but depending on the particular variety, shellfish may also be presented cooked. Mussels, never eaten raw, are often enjoyed steamed open in a simple white-wine and mussel broth (*moules marinières*) or bathed in a cream sauce. Lobster, crayfish (*langoustes*), crab (*crabes*), shrimp or prawns (*crevettes*) and larger scampi (*langoustines*) are also prepared in a variety of ways. Cephalopods such as squid (*encornet*) and cuttlefish (*seiche*) are fried or braised with vegetables. (See p. 54 for a recipe for *seiche aux poireaux*.) Octopus (*poulpe*) is added to salads, soups and stews.

Salad, once a transitional or restorative course before a cheese plate or dessert, is now found on menus as a starter dish. As a *grande salade,* it is a meal in itself, especially in more casual restaurants. *Salade niçoise,* named after the city of Nice, piled high with lettuce, string beans, hard-boiled eggs, capers and tuna, is a classic dating back to the early 1900s. Other examples are *frisée aux lardons* (curly endive with bacon and poached egg), *salade landaise* (with mushrooms and chicken gizzards, products associated with the Landes region of southwest France) and *salade norvégienne* (including Norwegian smoked salmon). French farmers grow many varieties of head lettuce, among them romaine, brought to France from Rome in the 14th century (hence its name), and *sucrine,* which resembles both romaine and butterhead lettuce. Mesclun, a mixture of young salad greens including arugula (*roquette*) and dandelion (*pissenlit*), is also commonly found. Lamb's lettuce (*mâche*) is a delicate-leaved green with a somewhat nutty flavor that is also popular in French salads.

Vegetables (*légumes*) play a significant role across French menus, especially with heightened interest in eating healthy, low-fat meals. Although vegetables may turn up as side dishes or garnishes along with the main course, they often figure prominently as dips and spreads, in soups, stews and savory tarts, or on their own, baked or stuffed. Rarely are vegetables just boiled, a style of cooking referred to as "in the English manner" (*à l'anglaise*). Vegetables are even ingredients in candies and desserts such as *tarte aux blettes*, which is made with Swiss chard.

The French tend to prefer white varieties of asparagus (*asperge*), which are grown under mounds of soil, blocked from sunlight. French radishes (*radis*) are often less sharp than American varieties and are eaten on buttered bread with coarse salt. The extensive use of herbs is a hallmark of French cookery. Many a French chef will have an herb garden (*potager*) in the backyard. It has been said that over 80 different varieties of edible mushrooms (*champignons*) grow wild in France, but cultivation is also big business. France is one of the world's foremost producers of cultivated mushrooms. Most commonly seen varieties are pale button mushrooms (*champignons de Paris*); porcini (*cèpes* or *bolets*); whitish oyster mushrooms (*pleurotes*); hedgehog mushrooms (*pieds-de-mouton*); creamy yellow chanterelles (*girolles*); and stubby, pocked morels (*morilles*). Dried seeds such as lentils (*lentilles*), chickpeas (*pois chiches*) and beans (*haricots*) are used extensively in dips, spreads, soups and side dishes.

Long, pink-and-white French Breakfast radishes, which are milder than red varieties commonly seen in the US, are eaten on French bread with unsalted butter and coarse salt.

Among the most prized ingredients in French cuisine is the truffle (*truffe*), reserved for festive dishes and associated with the kitchens of top-flight restaurants. But if one happens to have an oak tree in the backyard—seedlings are sold at food fairs for those eager to try their luck—and a truffle pig (or more likely a truffle dog), there may be enough of a harvest each year to feast upon more liberally. (See p. 46 for a recipe for *pâté de truffes façon Pierre Manin*.) Truffles are the stuff of legend, but plant biologists at the University of Nancy in northeastern France recently decoded the black truffle genome, uncovering some of its secrets. Perhaps of most significance is the discovery that the black truffle (the white truffle is found in Italy), once assumed to be asexual, actually has two sexes. Injecting oak tree roots with spores may enhance truffle growth and ultimately lower the price. Mapping truffle DNA may also establish differences from region to region and even lead to specific designations and protections similar to those given to particular wines and cheese.

Fruits do yeoman's service across France's culinary culture. They are the centerpiece in tarts, distilled into potent liqueurs, such as Calvados, Normandy's famous apple brandy, or pressed into juices and syrups. Fruits are essential ingredients in sweet soups and sauces, and are stewed with wine or liqueur into dessert compotes. (See p. 62 for a recipe for *cocotte de fruits au vin épicé avec diablotins aux amandes*.) Fruits are also the basis of extensive assortments of jellies and jams (*confitures*). France is one of Europe's largest producers of strawberries and kiwis, and southern France is one of the country's major fruit-producing areas. Two special fruits to look for are the diminutive Cavaillon melon and delicate Chasselas eating grapes.

Historically, soup has been at the core of the French diet. Soup was usually (and still is in some quarters) the main dish at the evening meal (*dîner* or *souper*), along with salad. At its simplest, soup can be nothing more than *potage,* a purée of garden vegetables cooked in water or broth, served with a piece of dry bread. At its most refined, it is a cream soup, such as *vichyssoise* (see recipe, p. 43) or seafood bisque. At its heartiest, soup can resemble a stew, a filling *mélange* of a region's bounty, such as the classic *bouillabaisse*.

France is the largest consumer of snails (*escargots*) in the world, although consumption has declined in recent years from reportedly 40,000 to about 20,000 tons annually. The large *escargot de Bourgogne* (*Helix pomatia*) is not farm-raised and is rarely found in France. More common are the *petit* (*Helix aspersa aspersa*) and *gros gris* (*Helix aspersa maxima*), which exist in both wild and cultivated varieties across France. The snails are washed, blanched and boiled, and their shells sterilized. They are then baked, usually in garlic butter and parsley.

Frog's legs (*cuisses de grenouille*) are, indeed, eaten in France, but the frogs rarely come from the shallows of France's freshwater lakes and streams. If they are not raised in artificial ponds, they are imported from China and central Europe. Typically, the upper part of the frog's hind leg

France is the world's largest consumer of snails (*escargots*) such as the *petit gris* (*Helix aspersa aspersa*), which is baked in garlic butter and served on special plates with tongs and tiny forks.

is floured, pan- or deep-fried in butter and garlic, and garnished with parsley and lemon slices. Other cooking preparations include frog's legs in soups or in a white-wine and cream sauce.

You don't have to be Italian to love pasta (*pâtes*). Pasta is frequently prepared in French households either as a side dish or a quick main course with the addition of vegetables and sauces. Although most rice (*riz*) is imported, red rice has been cultivated in southern France for several hundred years. (Plants were introduced from the Middle East by way of Italy and Spain.) Rice is appreciated in salads, as side dishes and in sweet puddings. There has been a renewed interest in ancient grains such as spelt (*épeautre*), which is used in soups and side dishes.

Waverly Root, in his masterful book, *The Food of France,* divided France by its cooking fats—butter (most of the West, North and East), fat (the center), olive oil (Provence) and a combination of all three (the Southwest). Today, these distinctions are not as clear-cut as French cooks around the country turn increasingly to monounsaturated fats. Olive oil production is significant in the south, but imports from other countries along the Mediterranean are also found. October and November are prime olive-harvest months in Provence. The olives are harvested by hand or machine, then washed, milled and pressed. But table olives may be available in September, once they have been cured. Familiar varieties are green *picholines* and small, black *niçoises*. Crushed green or black olives, mixed with capers and anchovies, make a delectable spread called *tapenade,* which is often sold in bulk at outdoor markets.

Sea salt (*fleur de sel*) was refined and harvested in France as early as 700 BCE, and has been vital to preserving meats and fish. Today, there are several main areas of sea salt production—the basins around the Île de Rey, Noirmourtier, Île d'Oléron and Guérande peninsula along the Atlantic coast; and in the Camargue marshes along the Mediterranean, east of Montpellier. The color of the salt varies from white to light gray, as does the taste, depending on the minerals contained in the salts. Mustard (*moutarde*) is another condiment that is a kitchen staple, although its use has been declining recently. It is mixed into salad dressings and sauces or spread on sausages, meats and fish. Once, France's mustard was ground from the seed of indigenous *Brassica* plants, but now most mustard seed is imported from North America. Mustard making once thrived in the Burgundy region, where it was linked to wine production, the crushed brown mustard seeds mixed with the juice of unripe grapes (*verjus*).

While mustard is still manufactured in Burgundy, production in Dijon ceased in 2009.

Most French people eat cheese, yogurt or fruit for dessert, but they take great pleasure in the occasional pastry (*pâtisserie*), especially on weekends. The French make a distinction between a bakery (*boulangerie*) and a pastry shop (*pâtisserie*), but they often do double-duty. Although most home cooks have several dessert recipes in their repertoire, they will often leave baking to the experts, especially when pressed for time or wanting to delight dinner guests. Most *pâtisseries* will offer an assortment of puffy pastries called *viennoiseries,* reflecting Vienna's earlier influence on French pastry making. *Croissants, pains au chocolat, pains aux raisins* and apple turnovers (*chaussons aux pommes*) are favorites, sometimes served to children at breakfast or after school as a treat.

The varieties of puddings, pies, cakes and cookies can be staggering, but there are a few standouts worth calling attention to. A much-loved cake country-wide is an Epiphany cake made of puff pastry and almond paste or almond cream (*galette des Rois*). Outside of the Christmas season this cake is known by the name *Pithiviers*. Other delectables are a custard-filled tart circled with caramelized cream puffs and named for the patron saint of bakers (*gâteau Saint-Honoré*); and, a two-crust pie filled with custard and jam (*gâteau Basque*) that is native to the Basque region in southwestern France. Fruit tarts are always big hits, whether baked with sugar, or piled fresh on top of pastry cream. Lemon tarts (*tartes au citron*), large and small, are among the most popular. The upside-down apple tart (*tarte Tatin*) is a bistro classic. (See p. 63 for a recipe for *tarte Tatin aux abricots*.)

Colorful macaroons (*macarons*), apparently devised several hundred years ago by nuns in eastern France, are in style. So are *cannelés de Bordeaux,* little caramelized cakes baked in special molds that give them a uniquely squat shape. And nothing is more sublime than Proust's beloved *madeleines,* small cakes baked in their familiar seashell shape. The French are great fans of

Epiphany cake (*galette des Rois*). A special favor (*fève*) is inserted into the almond paste filling, and whoever finds it in a slice is crowned king or queen.

chocolate, with a predilection for dark rather than milk chocolate. Shops specialize in the art of creating chocolates and other candies.

Foods with an A.O.C. status are clearly labeled. Another special stamp of quality to look for is Label Rouge, the red label given to hundreds of products. People concerned about organic food should keep an eye out for the green AB (*agriculture biologique*) etiquette, which authenticates the food as being raised according to government-defined standards.

The Regions of France

France is often called "The Hexagon" because of its six-sided geometry. The country is bordered on the north by Belgium and Luxemburg, and along the east by Germany, Switzerland and Italy. The Mediterranean Sea hugs France's southeast coast and the Pyrenees define the southwest where the country shares borders with Andorra and Spain. The Atlantic Ocean and the English Channel frame France to the west. Within the country, there is an extensive network of rivers and streams, including the country's major arteries—the Seine, the Loire, the Garonne and the Rhône.

France is a series of regions within regions, each of them particular and unique, and with good reason. France has one of the most varied geographies and variable climates on the European continent. The landscape is a series of contrasts, alternately smooth and rugged, intimate and overwhelming, with coastal plains and marshes, gentle rolling hills, lush forests, steep gorges and mountain ranges. The weather—temperate, oceanic, alpine and even tropical—makes it possible to have an extended growing season.

Despite modern transportation systems that make for easy distribution of foodstuffs nationwide, France continues to define food in regional terms. What one eats—where a particular butter, cheese, meat, fruit or vegetable comes from—can link French people to history and cultural heritage. France's regions represent identity, the place where old and new, the traditional and the contemporary, come not into conflict so much as into balance and harmony.

Although France has been organized administratively since the 1789 Revolution into departments—there are now nearly 100—people still refer to places using names of ancient provinces. Neat divisions are virtually impossible, and the word *pays* can sometimes best be translated not as "country" but "home." For convenience, we have divided France into seven regions with administrative districts given here in parentheses: the North/Northeast (Nord-Pas-de-Calais, Picardy, Champagne, Lorraine and Alsace); the East (Franche-Comté, Rhône-Alps and Burgundy); the South or Mediterranean France (Provence-Alps-Côte-d'Azur and the Languedoc-Roussillon); the Southwest (Midi-Pyrenees and Aquitaine); the West (Poitou-Charentes, Brittany, Normandy and Pays de la Loire); the Heartland (central France including the Limousin, Auvergne and Val-de-Loire) and the Île-de-France (Paris and suburbs).

The North and Northeast

France's northern coast is one of the country's most highly industrialized regions and a vital transportation corridor, featuring car-ferry terminals and the above-ground portion of the "Chunnel," the English Channel tunnel linking France to England by rail. Fish and shellfish are essential parts of the diet. Steamed mussels (*moules marinières*) are as popular here as they are in neighboring Belgium, and *waterzooi* is as much a French fish stew as it is Flemish. Inland, the area's flatlands have been wheat-growing areas, but also tragic battle- and burial grounds. Because of its climate, which is often cold and wet, the North is primarily beer not wine country, but champagne is the delightful and economically vital exception, even if it does not readily find its way into the North's generally robust cuisine. Hearty soups (such as *hochepot*, with meat and vegetables) and beer-flavored chicken, rabbit and beef stews are traditional. A terrine that may include any combination of rabbit, veal, chicken and pork (*potjeveleesh*), is a frequent menu item in Lille, as is pork sausage (*andouillette*) around Troyes. Gin is a main ingredient in *bistouille*, an invigorating coffee and chicory drink. Belgian endive, so-called because Belgian scientists developed and promoted it, is an important crop, exported widely. It is eaten raw in salads, stuffed and braised. Onions, squash and leeks are used to make a fine vegetable tart (*flamique* or *flamiche*). The North is not cow country so local cheeses are limited. An especially robust variety is Maroilles or Marolle, identified by its characteristic bright-orange washed rind. Chaource, a creamy cow's-milk cheese similar to Camembert, is produced in the Champagne.

Where the North's cooking hints at Belgium's influence, the Northeast's suggests German roots. Alsace and Lorraine were bitterly fought over for generations, alternately in French and German hands. But, despite the Germanic sounding names for several specialties—*kugelhopf* (yeast cake), *baeckeoffe* (a mixed meat stew), *presskopf* (a cold cut made from parts of pig's head), and *knoepfle* (noodles)—the cuisine is still very much French. Although this is pig-farming country where sausage-making is a fine art, a sauerkraut dish might just as readily be served with fish as with pork. Munster, a cow's-milk cheese with a reddish-orange rind, is the cheese of record. Sweet and savory tarts are specialties. *Flammeküche* (or *tarte flambée*), Alsace's version of pizza made from bread dough topped with bacon, onion and crème fraîche, is a favorite, as is *quiche lorraine,* made with eggs, cream, bacon or ham. Sweet custard tarts are dotted with yellow (*mirabelle*) and purple (*quetsche*) plums from the area's orchards. The fruits are vital for production of several highly touted liqueurs (*eaux-de-vie*). South of Strasbourg, a cosmopolitan city that is home to the European Parliament, vineyards are tucked between the west bank of the Rhine River and the Vosges Mountains. A host of white wines such as Riesling and Gewürtztraminer are grown here, reflected in dishes such as *poule au riesling,* a riff on Burgundy's *coq au vin* (see p. 50 for a recipe). Vittel and Contrex mineral waters are bottled in Alsace.

The East

Mountains define eastern France. The wooded elevations of the Jura in the Franche-Comté are succeeded by the rockier French Alps, including Mont Blanc, Europe's highest peak. Traditionally, the cooking in both the Franche-Comté and Rhône Alps (which includes the former provinces of Savoie and Dauphiné), has had the hallmarks of comfort food, a stick-to-the-ribs heaviness associated with colder climates. Milk from cows grazed on upland pastures has been used in a range of cheeses, such as Comté, an aged cow's-milk Gruyère- or Swiss-style cheese without holes; Morbier, with its characteristic middle layer of ash; Gex, a Roquefort-style cheese; and several different kinds of *tommes*. Cancoillotte is a popular cheese spread made from skim milk and butter; it is also a dish featuring the cheese paired with other ingredients. The area has long been famous for freshwater fish drawn from its rivers and lakes, such as the *omble chevalier* and *féra,* both in the salmon family. The Franche-Comté city of Nantua has given its name to a classic crayfish cream sauce served with creamed pike (*quenelles de brochet*), and the

Dauphiné is the namesake of a version of scalloped potatoes (*gratin dauphinois*; see recipe, p. 59). Among desserts, *pogne* turns from a squash pie in the eastern Dauphiné to something closer to a brioche in the west (see recipe, p. 65). The region produces several quality white wines, especially south of Lake Annecy, and liqueurs including Chartreuse. Evian mineral water is bottled on the French side of Lake Geneva.

Burgundy and the Lyonnais seem worlds away from the mountains, with a reputation for culinary excellence based on fine wine, beef, poultry and specialty foods. Lying to the west, Burgundy is a pleasant and fertile land of rolling hills that astonishingly can be green even in winter. Dominating the landscape are the famous vineyards along the chalky Côte d'Or, the gold coast south of Dijon, and the Beaujolais wine-producing district farther south roughly between Macon and Lyon. In addition to these reds and whites, Burgundy produces some light white wines in its northwestern corner, around the town of Chablis. Classic Burgundian dishes include roast rabbit in mustard sauce (*lapin rôti à la moutarde*), beef stew (*bœuf bourguignon;* see p. 48 for a recipe) and eggs poached in a thick red-wine sauce (*œufs en meurette*). Spice cake (*pain d'épices*; see recipe, p. 64) is aged for several weeks and sold in blocks, loaves, or small *nonettes*. Black currant liqueur (*crème de cassis*) is traditionally mixed with white wine (*aligoté*) for a Burgundian aperitif called *kir,* named after a former mayor of Dijon. Snails still keep their association with Burgundy, cooked in garlic butter. But beyond a few small snail farms in the region, most of the gastropods are imported. A noteworthy cow's-milk cheese is Époisses, which went out of production at the close of World War II but was revived in 1956. Also special are *poulet de Bresse* chicken and *jambon persillé,* ham in aspic. Flavigny-sur-Ozerain's anise-flavored candy and Lyon's almond pralines are specialty sweets.

The South or Mediterranean France

Provence, the sunlit country in the Midi, the south of France, stretches east from the Camargue wetlands and the Rhône River delta to France's border with Italy. Provence, from the Latin word for province, dips its feet into the Mediterranean Sea but rises north into hills scented with rosemary, lavender and thyme. This is the land that drew early Greek and Roman settlers looking for the good life. They brought olives and wine grapes, crops that still are

Confectionery is an art in France. In Burgundy's Flavigny-sur-Ozerain, sugar-coated aniseed candies (*pastilles*) date back hundreds of years and are the bonbon of choice.

important in the region's economic and social life. Olives get mashed into a flavorful olive spread (*tapenade*). Olive oil is the favored cooking medium. Garlic and tomatoes are two key ingredients in Provençal cuisine, with fish arguably running a close third. There are many different types of fish dishes in Provence, but fish soup (*soupe de poisson*) is ubiquitous. In Marseille, France's second-largest city, *bouillabaisse* has cult status, but different versions of this classic soup may be found up and down the coast. Purists insist on the addition of conger eel (*congre*), sea robin (*grondin*) and scorpion fish (*rascasse* or *chapon de mer*), a spiny, reddish-orange rockfish found in the Mediterranean's shallows. More expensive renditions will have lobster in the broth. Garlic is crushed into two main dips or sauces—*aïoli,* a mayonnaise that accompanies egg, vegetable, fish or meat dishes; and *rouille,* a saffron-colored mayonnaise added to soups. Vegetables are plentiful, with eggplant, zucchini, summer squash, peppers and tomatoes forming the basis of *ratatouille* and other vegetable stews called *tians* (see p. 60 for a recipe for *tian de courgettes et de tomates*), as well as savory tarts (see p. 46 for a recipe for *tarte de tomates et poivrons rouges*). Artichokes are a significant local crop. Among fruits, which are abundant, the small Cavaillon melon similar to honeydew is a specialty. *Fougasse,* a kind of foccacia sometimes studded with olives and anchovies, is found across the region. *Socca,* a flatcake or pancake made from a chickpea flour batter and baked in a large cast-iron pan, is served around Nice. Meat is not ignored in Provence, and beef and rabbit stews can be satisfying when the cold mistral wind blows in from the north. Banon, a goat's-milk cheese wrapped in chestnut leaves, is a familiar cheese in the region. As for sweets, the *calisson,* Aix-en-Provence's delightful diamond-shaped confection filled with almond paste, is now sold across France. The same is true of nougat, but Montélimar in the Rhône valley still claims to be the honey candy's capital.

Southern France was once Occitania and its inhabitants spoke a medieval language called Occitan, the *langue d'oc, oc* meaning "yes." (The *langue d'oui* took root in the northern half of the country and evolved into modern French.) Today, the Languedoc represents a much smaller region. It is immediately west of the Rhône River, its coastal plains set alongside the Mediterranean Sea. The land rises into herb-scented scrubland (*garrigue*) and extends northward to the rugged mountains of the Cévennes. Adjoining the Languedoc to the south, along France's frontier with Spain, is the Roussillon, Catalan country. The two districts are often hyphenated and referred to in one breath as the Languedoc-Roussillon.

The eastern Languedoc is olive-growing country, and its valleys are lively production centers for wine, fruits and vegetables, all of which figure prominently in the diet. But a range of fish and shellfish, cooked together in chowders or served as stand-alone dishes, are mainstays across the area. Mussels and oysters are farmed around the Mediterranean port of Bouzigues in the Languedoc; anchovies and sardines come ashore to the south in the Roussillon town of Collioure. Several communes surrounding Collioure produce a fortified aperitif or dessert wine called Banuyls, which is similar to Port.

An 18th-century illustration of a *rascasse*, from *Allgemeine Naturgeschichte der Fische* by Marcus Elieser Bloch. Courtesy of the Department of Special Collections, Memorial Library, University of Wisconsin–Madison.

The Southwest

The Pyrenees serve as the backdrop for a variety of culinary cultures across territory still referred to by the ancient name Gascony, although the contemporary administrative labels are Midi-Pyrenees and Aquitaine. Gascony stretches from roughly Toulouse west to Bordeaux, which lies along the Garonne, one of the region's two great rivers. The other, the Dordogne, is a gateway to the Périgord, land of walnuts, geese and truffles. Both the Garonne and Dordogne meet at the Gironde estuary, an important transportation corridor between the Atlantic and the interior.

In Gascony, raising geese and ducks is an important industry. The poultry, and especially their fattened livers, are sold at specialized markets (*marchés au gras*). Confits of goose (*d'oie*) and duck (*de canard*)—birds cooked and preserved in their own fat—are regular items on menus, as are plump pieces of foie gras. Cornmeal, prepared as a mush (*mique* or *millas*), is fried in goose fat. Game is transformed into rich pâtés. Milk-fed lamb from Pauillac is renowned. One of the region's emblematic dishes is *cassoulet,* a meat stew where the common denominator is dried beans. Location and the inclination of the cook determine the rest of the ingredients, among them sausage, mutton, and preserved goose or duck. Bordeaux's world-class wines and Armagnac liqueur add flavor to many a dish. Seafood is plentiful. Oysters are harvested in lagoons along the Atlantic coast at Arcachon, south of Bordeaux. The cooking changes in the southwestern corner along the Atlantic, in the Basque country (Pays Basque) bordering Spain. Here, red pepper is a frequent ingredient in regional dishes. Peppers grown around the village of Espelette are dried into *piment d'Espelette,* a spice similar to paprika used for flavoring and curing meats. The preparation of delicatessen meats (*charcuterie*) is a noble art and Bayonne ham is a specialty. The Atlantic leaves its mark on Basque cookery, especially in fish chowder (*ttoro*). Among the noteworthy desserts is *gâteau Basque,* a two-crust tart filled with custard and jam.

The West

The Atlantic Ocean defines western France, from the salt marshes of the Poitou-Charentes northward to the rugged coastline of Brittany and Normandy's sandy beaches. Clay along the Breton riverbanks at Quimper

Glazed pottery (*faïence*) is a specialty of Quimper in Brittany, where china is hand-painted with scenes of village life and villagers in traditional dress.

encouraged a lively tin-glazed pottery industry, with hand-painted figures reflecting centuries of village history, life and dress. Fish and shellfish—especially mussels and oysters farmed here extensively—are economic drivers. Fish stews are ubiquitous, although their names and ingredients vary from place to place. The Poitou-Charentes' *chaudrée* is made with eel, plaice and sole, but Brittany's *cotriade* is filled with onions and potatoes as well as the local catch. In the south, mussels are cooked in a curry-flavored cream sauce (*mouclade*) but are more simply steamed in cider farther north.

The region's interior is largely agricultural, growing fruits and vegetables, especially artichokes, cabbage, onions and cauliflower. The forests and streams of the Loire Valley, once royal hunting grounds, still supply freshwater fish, and deer and waterfowl are the makings for rich terrines, roasts and stews. Cattle and pig farming are important. Lamb from animals that graze along the salt marshes is especially prized, and pork spread (*rillettes*) is shipped from Tours across France. Normandy is dairy and apple country. Some of France's best butters, creams and cheeses come to life here, including Livarot, Neufchâtel and Camembert. In Normandy, apples are pressed into cider and distilled into Calvados. Normandy is also the locus of production of another liqueur, Benedictine, made from spices, plants and a base of Cognac, itself a product of Poitou-Charentes. Among the desserts, Normandy's apple tarts are legend, as are Brittany's crêpes, a buttery cake (*gâteau breton*), and a stodgier but satisfying prune pudding (*far breton*).

The Heartland

Deep France, or *la France profonde*, is a term that can refer to any number of places that seem away from it all and, by virtue of their isolation, authentically French. Perhaps no spot better qualifies as the heartland than the Auvergne and Limousin, tucked away in the center of the country, earthy, unaffected and, until recently, remote. Geologically, this is one of the oldest parts of the Hexagon, a region of extinct volcanoes (*puys*), eerie deposits of volcanic stone, the Massif Central's mountains and high plateaus, and weather that alternately can be sweltering or bitterly cold. This is good ground for raising sheep and cattle. The cooking is hearty, with an emphasis on meat and potatoes, cheese and garlic, chestnuts, walnuts and lentils, especially those from Le Puy. Two of the region's signature dishes are a hot pot of pork and vegetables, including cabbage, (*potée auvergnate*) and mashed potatoes with cheese (*aligot*). Among the most well-known cheeses are Cantal, a hard cow's-milk cheese, formed into enormous blocks, and two blue cheeses made from cow's milk—Bleu d'Auvergne and Fourme d'Ambert. The region is a solid producer of fruit, especially cherries, which are the essential ingredients in a pudding called *clafoutis*.

The Île-de-France

You might say that France comes together in the Île-de-France, the Island of France. Several rivers circle it, and the River Seine runs through it. For generations, Paris and the surrounding metropolitan area have drawn people from every corner of the country. Paris is the Hexagon's political and economic heart. It is also the center of France's culinary heritage. Chefs and restaurateurs who have left the provinces seeking their fortunes in the big city proudly dish up home cooking. The names of some of their establishments—Le Languedoc, Au Trou Gascon, for example—testify to their roots. Not only is the cooking of France accessible in Paris, the cuisine of the country's overseas departments and former colonies can be enjoyed here, too—the West Indies (Antilles), Southeast Asia, North, West and Central Africa.

Because Paris has been the seat of money and power for centuries, it has been France's culinary trendsetter, the "in" place where new inventions have taken flight. Restaurants got their start here over 200 years ago. Haute cuisine was born along the banks of the Seine. The city still continues to nurture young, experimental chefs looking to bend the old ways but also lets traditional cooking hold its ground. It is worth remembering that before urban sprawl, the Île-de-France was a breadbasket and significant food supplier. The region produced fruits and vegetables, wines and cheeses—vineyards grew where the Eiffel Tower now stands—and the region still remains a great provider. Hundreds of thousands of tons of foodstuffs are shipped annually across the European continent from Rungis, the huge wholesale market south of the city.

Paris has been accused of having nothing rightfully to call its own. More likely, dishes that originated here traveled, and, as they did, their beginnings were forgotten or ignored. But Paris just might lay claim to *matelote,* a stew of freshwater fish cooked in onions, mushrooms and wine. Several soups can be said to be Parisian, including *potage parisienne,* made from leeks, carrots and potatoes, and *potage Saint-Germain,* a pea soup. *Vol-au-vent* puff pastry cases filled with cream sauces were popularized here. Little button mushrooms and Brie cheeses come from the Île-de-France. Nineteenth-century stars of the kitchen get credit for dreaming up classics that whisper, "Paris." *Potage Germiny,* an egg and sorrel soup, was created for the Comte Germiny by Adolphe Dugléré at the Café des Anglais; pressed duck rose to culinary heights at the Tour d'Argent; and *sole Marguery* served with shrimp came to life at Restaurant Marguery. And what dishes currently being hatched will be as quintessentially Parisian as these?

Tastes of France

You are encouraged to try some of these classic and new French recipes before you leave home. This is a wonderful and immediately rewarding way to preview the cuisine of France. Most of the ingredients necessary for these recipes are available in the United States (see *Resources,* p. 71). Satisfactory substitutes are given for those that may be unavailable.

SOUPS

Vichyssoise

Potato and leek soup. Serves 8.

French chef Louis Diat is credited with inventing this luxurious chilled soup at New York's Ritz-Carlton. Diat claims he came up with the recipe in the summer of 1917 as he was reflecting on the dish his family used to eat in his hometown of Montmarault, near Vichy, in central France (although a similar soup appears in a 19th-century cookbook). Whatever the origin, *vichyssoise* has become a classic. This recipe comes from chef Liane Kuony, who was my cooking teacher. For many years, Kuony, who died in 2005, was the proprietor of the renowned Postilion Restaurant, School of Culinary Arts and Studio of Interior Design in Fond du Lac, Wisconsin.

  3–4 LEEKS, WHITE AND TENDER GREEN PARTS ONLY

  ½ POUND ONION (ABOUT 1 LARGE ONION), CHOPPED

  1¾ POUNDS POTATOES (ABOUT 4 LARGE), PEELED

  4 TABLESPOONS UNSALTED BUTTER

  4 CUPS CHICKEN STOCK

  1½ CUPS MILK*

  2½ CUPS HEAVY (WHIPPING) CREAM*

  SALT AND WHITE PEPPER TO TASTE

  CHIVES FOR GARNISH

Wash and clean the leeks. Cut into thin slices. Remove all brown spots and eyes from the potatoes and dice them. Melt the butter in a large frying pan and add the

[Vichyssoise, *continued*]

leeks. Cook them over medium heat, making sure they remain glossy and translucent. If the heat is too high and you brown the leeks, you will have to start again. When the leeks are thoroughly coated with butter, add the onions and continue to cook slowly over low to medium heat for 10 minutes. Set aside.

In a large (4-quart) casserole or Dutch oven, warm the chicken stock and add the leeks, onions and diced potatoes. Cook the soup over low heat for 30 minutes to an hour or until the potatoes are cooked. Let the soup cool briefly. When it is not too hot to handle, ladle the soup in batches into a blender. Purée the soup until smooth, then pour it through a strainer into a ceramic or glass (not metal) bowl to eliminate any fibrous parts of the leeks. Repeat with the other batches. Gently stir in the milk and cream as the soup cools. Cover with plastic wrap and refrigerate for several hours until cold.

Before serving, taste the soup for seasoning; add salt and white pepper as needed. Ladle the soup into bowls and decorate with snipped chives.

*The soup is best with whole milk and cream but it is still pleasurable with 2% milk and equal parts heavy cream and half-and-half to reduce the amount of saturated fat.

Soupe à l'Ail Nouveau

New garlic soup. Serves 4.

Susan Herrmann Loomis's soup is a beautifully simple dish, with delicate flavors and a smooth, sophisticated finish—even a restrained kind of sweetness. You must use fresh garlic, available in the springtime or early summer. Loomis, who holds dual American and French citizenship, is the author of several cookbooks and a memoir, *On Rue Tatin*. She lives and teaches cooking in Normandy.

> 3 LARGE OR 4 MEDIUM HEADS OF NEW GARLIC
>
> 1 SMALL (4-OUNCE) STARCHY POTATO
>
> ½ TEASPOON FINE SEA SALT
>
> 2½ CUPS WATER
>
> ONE 4-INCH LENGTH OF FRESH ROSEMARY
>
> 1 LARGE EGG, SEPARATED
>
> CHERVIL FOR GARNISH

Separate and peel the garlic cloves. Peel and dice the potato. Place the garlic cloves, potato, salt, water and rosemary in a medium-sized saucepan and bring the ingredients to a boil over medium-high heat. Cover. Reduce the heat to medium-low so that the water is barely simmering. Cook until the potato is tender and the garlic is soft all the way through, about 30 minutes. Remove the rosemary and purée the soup in a food processor. Taste for seasoning. In a bowl, whisk the egg white until it is frothy and soft peaks are about to form.

Return the soup to the stove and bring it just to the boiling point. Whisk in the egg yolk until it is thoroughly combined and the soup thickens slightly, then whisk in the egg white until it is thoroughly combined and the soup is frothy. Remove from the heat. For a perfectly smooth soup free of garlic threads, strain the soup through a sieve. Or simply serve, garnished with chervil.

APPETIZERS OR FIRST COURSES

Biscuits de Langoustine

Crayfish flan. Serves 4.

Adapted from Catherine and Patrick Auduc's recipe. The Auducs are proprietors of La Vieille Auberge, in Saulieu, Burgundy. Although the dish is called "biscuits," no pastry is involved. The flan, however, might remind some people of the softness of sponge cake. While *langoustine*—a small lobster-style crustacean or crayfish—is not easy to find in the US, medium-sized shrimp or bite-sized slices of lobster tail can be used as a substitute. The dish can be served as an appetizer or as a first course with a salad.

> 10 OUNCES OF WHITING, COD OR TURBOT*
>
> 3 LARGE EGGS, BEATEN
>
> 1¼ CUPS HEAVY CREAM
>
> ¼–½ TEASPOON NUTMEG
>
> ¼–½ TEASPOON SALT
>
> WHITE PEPPER TO TASTE
>
> 1–2 TABLESPOONS BUTTER TO GREASE RAMEKINS
>
> 4 CRAYFISH†
>
> LETTUCE LEAVES (OPTIONAL)
>
> SLICES OF LEMON (OPTIONAL)

In a food processor, process the fish meat for a few seconds—about ten pulses—until smooth. Combine the fish with the beaten eggs, cream, nutmeg, salt and white pepper. Lightly butter four 1-cup ramekins. Fill each ramekin about two-thirds full with the fish mixture. Insert a crayfish, shrimp or piece of lobster tail into each ramekin. Place the ramekins in a baking dish. Make a *bain-marie* by pouring boiling water into the baking dish about halfway up the sides of the ramekins. Bake for about 45 minutes at 325°F until the custard is set. Cool 5–10 minutes before unmolding. To unmold each ramekin, run a knife around the edge, place a serving plate on top and invert it, giving it a good shake to release the custard. Serve lukewarm or chilled, plain or with a shellfish or tomato sauce.

*Other white, soft-textured fish may be substituted.

†Medium-sized shrimp or pieces of lobster tail, shells removed, may be substituted.

Pâté de Truffes Façon Pierre Manin

Pierre Manin's truffle spread.

My friend Pierre Manin makes this spread every fall from truffles he and a neighbor's truffle dog find under Pierre's live oaks in the Dauphiné region of east-central France. For this recipe, use a 3-to-1 ratio of butter to truffles. Yes, truffles are expensive. But make this a special treat.

DEMI-SEL OR SALTED, EUROPEAN-STYLE BUTTER

BEST-QUALITY TRUFFLES, VERY FINELY CHOPPED

FRENCH BREAD, THINLY SLICED AND TOASTED, BUT NOT TOO CRISP

Soften the butter so that it is easy to cream. Gradually whip the truffles into the butter until they are completely incorporated. Place the spread in a small ramekin, cover with plastic wrap and refrigerate until hard. Serve with the toast.

Tarte de Tomates et Poivrons Rouges

Tomato and red pepper tart. Serves 6.

This recipe comes from chef Peter Shaw and his wife, Sally. Together, they run Here on the Spot, a catering business in the south of France that also offers luxury gourmet food holidays and cooking classes. Peter's cuisine, which he calls "Mediterranean Rim," imaginatively illustrates what can happen when an English-born chef comes under the influence of the culinary traditions and culture of the Languedoc-Roussillon region. This dish resembles *pissaladière,* the classic French-style pizza native to southeastern France (see *Menu Guide*). To make this tart substituting pizza dough, see recipe, p. 67. You can also use the filling in a two-crust tart made with puff pastry. The filling can also be served simply as a vegetable dish, without the anchovies.

Herb crust

1–2 TEASPOONS PLUS ⅓ CUP EXTRA-VIRGIN OLIVE OIL

2 CUPS ALL-PURPOSE FLOUR

⅔ CUP GRATED PARMESAN CHEESE

2 TEASPOONS SALT

1 TABLESPOON HERBES DE PROVENCE*

2 LARGE CLOVES OF GARLIC, FINELY CHOPPED

4–7 TABLESPOONS WATER

Filling

1 POUND, 12 OUNCES RIPE PLUM TOMATOES†

2 TABLESPOONS EXTRA-VIRGIN OLIVE OIL

4 MEDIUM ONIONS, FINELY SLICED

2 CLOVES OF GARLIC, FINELY CHOPPED

2 MEDIUM RED PEPPERS, SEEDED AND SLICED

1 TABLESPOON TOMATO PASTE

12 BLACK OLIVES, PITTED, CUT IN HALF

1 TABLESPOON SUGAR

2 TEASPOONS OREGANO

SALT AND BLACK PEPPER TO TASTE

1 CAN OF ANCHOVY FILLETS (OPTIONAL)

ADDITIONAL OLIVES (OPTIONAL)

1 TABLESPOON CHOPPED PARSLEY FOR GARNISH

Lightly grease a 9 × 2" tart pan (with removable bottom) with 1–2 teaspoons olive oil. Sift the flour into a bowl and mix in the Parmesan cheese, salt and herbs. Set aside. In a small skillet or saucepan, sauté the garlic in ⅓ cup olive oil over medium heat for 2 minutes. Remove from the heat. Add 4 tablespoons of water and stir to combine the oil and water. Pour the hot mixture into the flour and knead the dough (or pulse in a food processor) just until it comes together. Add more water if necessary, 1 tablespoon at a time. Roll the dough out between two sheets of waxed paper. The dough should be no more than ¼" thick and wide enough to fit into the tart pan. If the dough crumbles and is difficult to roll out, use your hands to press the dough into the pan. Prick the dough with a fork at 2" intervals to keep it from rising in the oven. Cover with waxed paper or plastic wrap and refrigerate for 20 minutes. Preheat the oven to 400°F. Place the tart pan on a baking sheet and bake for 25 minutes or until firm. Remove from oven. Set aside until ready to use.

While the tart shell is baking, make the filling. If using fresh tomatoes, make an incision at the base of each tomato and blanch for about 1 minute in boiling water, or until the skin begins to separate. Remove the tomatoes to a large bowl of cold water and remove the skin. On a cutting board, slice the tomatoes in half, remove the seeds and chop the tomato flesh. If using canned tomatoes, strain and chop. Place olive oil in a large frying pan over medium heat. Add the onions, garlic and peppers, and cook them until soft, but not browned—about 10 minutes. Add the prepared tomatoes, tomato paste, olives, sugar, oregano, salt and pepper to the pan and cook over medium heat until all the liquid has evaporated. Pour the filling into the tart shell, smoothing the top with a spatula. Decorate the top of the tart with the anchovies in a crosshatch design. Place an olive wherever the anchovies intersect. Reduce the oven temperature to 200°F and bake for 15 more minutes. When the tart has cooled, transfer it to a serving plate by removing the sides of the tart pan. You can also remove the bottom with a spatula or the base of another tart mold. Sprinkle with chopped parsley and serve.

*A mix of some or all of the following may be substituted: ground fennel, basil, savory, thyme and rosemary.

†Canned tomatoes (28 ounces) may be substituted.

Verrine de Crème d'Avocat
Avocado cream. Serves 4.

This recipe comes from chef François Deduit, proprietor of the Hostellerie du Moulin Fouret, in Normandy. It was swamp and ruin when Chef Deduit bought it 25 years ago. He has lovingly turned it into a restaurant and inn with a spectacular garden and trout stream. Chef Deduit serves this dish in *verrines* or small glasses as an accompaniment to a smoked salmon entrée (see recipe, p. 52). The avocado cream, however, can stand by itself. It should be made just before serving, as the avocado loses its attractive green color with time.

2 AVOCADOS, PERFECTLY RIPE

4 TABLESPOONS CRÈME FRAÎCHE

2–3 TEASPOONS LEMON JUICE

LEAFY TOP OF A FENNEL BULB

SEA SALT

In a food processor, process the avocados until they are perfectly smooth. Add crème fraîche. If there are any visible lumps, push the avocado cream through a moderately fine sieve. Add lemon juice and stir to combine. Put the avocado cream in a pastry bag without a tip and pipe the cream into four small *verrines,* about 2" wide and 3" deep, or other small serving glasses. Decorate with fennel. Sprinkle the top with a pinch of sea salt. Serve immediately.

Main Dishes

Bœuf Bourguignon
Burgundian beef stew. Serves 8.

This version of the classic dish comes from the late Liane Kuony. For many years, Kuony was the proprietor of the renowned Postilion Restaurant, School of Culinary Arts and Studio of Interior Design in Fond du Lac, Wisconsin. Well before many Midwestern chefs—pros and amateurs alike—were cooking with the seasons, Kuony promoted locally grown produce and forged relationships with area farmers, encouraging them to raise special (and healthy) animals and crops.

6 OUNCES SALT PORK OR SLAB BACON, DICED

4 POUNDS CHUCK STEAK, FAT TRIMMED AWAY, CUT IN 1½-INCH CUBES*

CANOLA OIL, APPROXIMATELY 4 TABLESPOONS, DIVIDED

1½ POUNDS ONIONS, QUARTERED

3 CLOVES GARLIC, MINCED

2 POUNDS CARROTS, WASHED (UNPEELED), BIAS CUT INTO 1½-INCH CUBES

¾ POUND SMALL BUTTON MUSHROOMS, CUT IN HALF

¾ CUP ALL PURPOSE FLOUR

1 QUART BEEF STOCK, WARMED BUT NOT HOT

1 BOTTLE RED WINE, SUCH AS A BURGUNDY

BOUQUET GARNI OF SEVERAL SPRIGS OF FRESH PARSLEY AND THYME

2 BAY LEAVES

1 TABLESPOON SALT

1 TABLESPOON FRESH BLACK PEPPER

Bring water to boil in a small saucepan and blanch the diced salt pork for about 2 minutes, or until it is white. Drain in a sieve and then fry in a large (7-quart) casserole or Dutch oven, until the meat is browned. Remove and drain on paper towels. Set aside. In the remaining fat in the casserole, brown the chuck steak cubes in batches. If there is not enough oil remaining, add 1–2 tablespoons of canola oil. Do not crowd the meat. It should brown, not stew. Remove the browned meat to a large bowl.

Add onions and garlic to the casserole, again adding more canola oil if needed. Sauté the onions until they are translucent, about 3–4 minutes. Add the carrots and mushrooms.

Return the beef to the pot, along with the pork cracklings. Sift flour over the meat in increments, adding some of the beef stock as you go, making sure that the flour does not form lumps. Add red wine, the bouquet garni, bay leaves, salt and pepper. Preheat the oven to 375°F. Place the pot, uncovered, in the oven. When the stew begins to boil, reduce the temperature to 325°F. Cook for about 2 hours or until the meat is extremely tender and the carrots are soft. Remove the bouquet garni and bay leaves before serving. The dish can be prepared ahead of time and reheated.

*Organic or pasture-raised beef is preferable.

Filet de Loup à l'Aneth et Pastis
Fillet of sea bass with dill and pastis. Serves 2.

This dish is adapted from one prepared by Bridget Pugh, Executive Chef of Le Bistro à Vin in Montpeyroux in the Languedoc-Roussillon. As her name suggests, Pugh is not French. She is a former ballerina from New Zealand but has been hailed as one of the area's more audacious and inspired chefs.

VINAIGRETTE (SEE RECIPE, P. 66)

1–2 SMALL YELLOW SQUASH

2–3 SMALL ZUCCHINI

1 SMALL JICAMA, PEELED

6 OIL-CURED BLACK OLIVES

[Filet de Loup à l'Aneth et Pastis, *continued*]

> YOUNG, THIN ASPARAGUS TIPS (OPTIONAL)
>
> TWO 5-OUNCE FILLETS OF SEA BASS OR SIMILAR FISH, WITH THE SKIN ON
>
> 2 TABLESPOONS WHITE WINE
>
> 2 TABLESPOONS OLIVE OIL
>
> FRESH DILL, WASHED AND DRIED

Prepare the vinaigrette and set aside. Julienne the vegetables, finely dice the olives and set aside. Preheat the oven to 400°F. Sprinkle the flesh side of the fish fillets with white wine. Place flesh side down on a non-stick baking sheet and paint the skin lightly with olive oil. Bake about 5 minutes or until firm to the touch at the thickest part. While the fish is baking, steam the vegetables for 3–5 minutes. When the fish and vegetables are done, place the vegetables in the middle of the serving platter or individual plates, pour on a few tablespoons of the vinaigrette, and top with the fish fillet(s). Decorate the plate with dill and diced black olives.

Coq au Vin

Chicken or capon in red wine. Serves 8.

Jean-Luc Evenas, the chef at Les Routiers, a bistro in Paris's 18th arrondissement or district, prepared this dish for me. Evenas and Les Routiers' owners, Bernard and Joëlle Dubreuil, serve traditional dishes, prepared the old-fashioned way, with a commitment to cooking from scratch. Before the city's *périphérique,* or ring road, was built, the bistro was a truck stop on a main artery into the city and its central market, Les Halles. Les Routiers still has a loyal neighborhood clientele.

> 1 CHICKEN OR CAPON, ABOUT 4 POUNDS, CUT INTO 8 PIECES*
>
> 3 TABLESPOONS OLIVE OIL
>
> 3 TABLESPOONS UNSALTED BUTTER
>
> SALT AND FRESHLY GROUND BLACK PEPPER
>
> 2–3 MEDIUM ONIONS, PEELED AND SLICED
>
> ¾ CUP FLOUR
>
> BOUQUET GARNI OF PARSLEY, THYME AND 2 BAY LEAVES
>
> 1 BOTTLE DRY BUT FRUITY RED WINE, SUCH AS A BURGUNDY
>
> ½ CUP WATER (OR CHICKEN STOCK), OR ENOUGH TO COVER THE CHICKEN
>
> 2 LARGE CLOVES GARLIC, WHOLE
>
> 1 POUND CARROTS, PEELED AND SLICED INTO 1-INCH PIECES
>
> ½ POUND SMALL BUTTON MUSHROOMS, CUT IN HALF

Pat the chicken pieces dry. In a large (5-quart) casserole or Dutch oven, heat 2 tablespoons each of olive oil and butter, reserving the remaining tablespoon of each for cooking the mushrooms. When the oil begins to bubble, add the chicken pieces, skin side down, being careful not to crowd the pan. Sauté the chicken pieces on one side until they are lightly golden, salt and pepper them, then turn them over and repeat, cooking about 5 minutes on each side. When golden, remove the chicken pieces to a plate.

Sauté the onions in the same pan until they are translucent, about 4 minutes. Sift about ½–¾ cup of flour into the onions, stirring to make sure the flour does not clump. Return the chicken and any juices to the pot, placing the breast pieces on top. Pour the wine over the chicken. Add water or chicken stock to barely cover the chicken. Bring the liquid just to a boil, lower the heat and simmer, covered, for about 2 hours.

About 30 minutes before you are ready to serve the chicken, add the garlic and carrots. With the remaining tablespoon each of butter and olive oil, sauté the mushrooms for a few minutes in a separate frying pan, and add to the pot 10 minutes before serving. If the sauce is too thin, ladle ½–1 cup of liquid into a small bowl and sift 2–4 tablespoons of flour into the broth, whisking until it thickens. Then return the mixture to the pot. Remove the bouquet garni. Serve the dish with boiled potatoes or noodles.

Variation: If you wish, you may begin making the dish with ¼ pound of slab bacon, cut into ½" dice. Sauté the bacon in the Dutch oven until golden, then remove and drain on paper towels. Reserve the bacon pieces to sprinkle over the dish just before serving. Strain off the bacon fat, or use it, along with the olive oil, to brown the chicken. Evenas doesn't brown the chicken in bacon fat or flame it with a few tablespoons of cognac before adding the wine. But you can.

*A capon, or neutered rooster, is preferable to chicken because it is bigger and more flavorful. Traditionally, cooks used an old bird that had just about outlived its usefulness on the farm but was prime meat for stewing.

Lapin à l'Oseille

Rabbit stew with sorrel. Serves 4.

Food journalist Susan Herrmann Loomis is the author of numerous cookbooks, including *The French Farmhouse Cookbook*. She demonstrated how to make this dish at her cooking school in Normandy.

    1 TABLESPOON EXTRA-VIRGIN OLIVE OIL (OPTIONAL)

    5 OUNCES SLAB BACON, RIND REMOVED, CUT INTO 1 × ½-INCH PIECES

    1 MEDIUM RABBIT (ABOUT 3½ POUNDS), CUT INTO 6 PIECES*

    FINE SEA SAT AND FRESHLY GROUND BLACK PEPPER

    1 POUND ONIONS

    1 CUP DRY WHITE WINE, SUCH AS A SAUVIGNON BLANC

    2 FRESH BAY LEAVES

[Lapin à l'Oseille, *continued*]

4 CUPS LOOSELY PACKED SORREL LEAVES

1 CUP CRÈME FRAÎCHE OR HEAVY (WHIPPING) CREAM†

If the bacon is very lean, you will need to use the olive oil. Heat the oil, if using, in a large, heavy pan (with 3" sides) over medium heat. Add the bacon and sauté until it is golden on all sides. Remove the bacon with a slotted spoon and set it aside. Drain all but 1 tablespoon of the fat from the pan. Add as many pieces of the rabbit as will comfortably fit in the pan without crowding. Sprinkle with salt and pepper and brown until golden, about 5 minutes on each side. Repeat until all the pieces are browned. Set the rabbit aside.

Peel the onions, cut in half crosswise and slice paper-thin. Add the onions to the pan and cook, stirring until they are softened, about 8 minutes. Add the wine and scrape any browned bits from the bottom of the pan. Return the rabbit and bacon to the pan along with the bay leaves, pushing the rabbit down among the onions. Bring to a boil, then reduce the heat to medium. Cover and cook at a lively simmer until the rabbit is tender and nearly cooked through, about 30 minutes.

While the rabbit is cooking, rinse the sorrel leaves, pat dry, and remove the stems. Stack the sorrel leaves on a cutting board and cut crosswise into very thin strips (chiffonnade). Remove the rabbit to a platter, cover it loosely with aluminum foil, and keep it warm in a low oven. Bring the pan's cooking juices to a boil over medium-high heat. Reduce the liquid by two-thirds, then stir in the cream. Bring the sauce just to a boil, then lower the heat so that the cream stays at a lively simmer. Cook until the sauce is reduced by about one-third. Add the sorrel, stirring as it melts down into the sauce. Adjust the seasoning.

Remove the rabbit from the oven. Drain away any juices. Warm the rabbit pieces in the cream sauce until heated through, about 5 minutes. Transfer the rabbit pieces to a warmed platter or shallow bowl. Pour sauce on top and serve immediately.

*Two back legs, two body pieces, two shoulder and front leg pieces. If the body is in a single piece, bone out the meat and tie it together with twine.

†Do not use ultrapasteurized products.

Pannequet de Saumon Fumé

Smoked salmon "wrap" with trout eggs. Serves 4.

This dish is adapted from a recipe by François Deduit at the Hostellerie du Moulin Fouret, Normandy. Deduit smokes his own salmon, wraps it around chopped *bulots,* or sea snails, and tops it off with trout eggs. This version uses lightly sautéed small cucumbers and shallots, which evoke the crunchy quality of the bulots, although not their special taste. This dish can be served with *verrine de crème d'avocat* (see recipe, p. 48).

4 LARGE SLICES SMOKED SALMON, PREFERABLY WILD

4 SMALL CUCUMBERS (2 INCHES LONG)

UNSALTED BUTTER OR OLIVE OIL (ABOUT 2 TABLESPOONS)

2–4 TABLESPOONS CRÈME FRAÎCHE

HEAVY CREAM

4 TEASPOONS TROUT ROE (OR OTHER FISH EGGS), FRESH OR BOTTLED

4 TEASPOONS FRESH LEMON JUICE

SEA SALT

LEAFY TOPS OF A FENNEL BULB OR FRESH CHIVES

Finely dice the cucumbers and sauté gently in butter or olive oil until they become slightly translucent but not soft, about 2 minutes. Set aside. Mix a few tablespoons of crème fraîche with enough heavy cream to make the crème fraîche liquid. Set aside. When you are ready to serve guests, place equal servings of cucumber on each diner's plate and cover the cucumber snugly with a piece of smoked salmon. Place a teaspoon of trout eggs on top of the salmon. To finish the dish, sprinkle a teaspoon of lemon juice and a pinch of sea salt on each serving of salmon and eggs. Decorate the plate with the crème fraîche mixture. Top the salmon with the leafy tops of a fennel bulb or snipped chives.

Porcelet Rôti au Jus avec Radis Confits et Petites Carottes
Roast pork with glazed radishes and baby carrots. Serves 6.
This recipe is adapted from a dish by Frédéric Ménager, chef at La Ruchotte, a Burgundian farmhouse inn and restaurant he and his wife, Eva, opened in 2001 near Bligny-sur-Ouche, outside of Beaune. Ménager had worked in the kitchens of Michelin-starred chefs, including Pierre Gagnaire, but he had a passion for the land, farming organically, and raising heritage breeds of chicken. With rare exceptions, the food served at his table is produced on the farm.

1 PORK SHOULDER (PREFERABLY BONE-IN)*

2–3 TABLESPOONS SUNFLOWER OR CANOLA OIL

2 ONIONS

3 LARGE CARROTS

5 CLOVES GARLIC, UNPEELED

ABOUT 20 BABY CARROTS†

ABOUT 20 FRENCH BREAKFAST RADISHES††

2–3 TABLESPOONS BUTTER OR OLIVE OIL

SALT AND WHITE PEPPER

1–2 TEASPOONS SUGAR

[Porcelet Rôti au Jus avec Radis Confits et Petites Carottes, *continued*]
Preheat oven to 350°F. Wash and dry the meat and rub it with a little salt. Put the cooking oil in a metal roasting pan large enough to hold the meat and the vegetables, and warm it on the stove. Add the pork shoulder and brown lightly on all sides. Coarsely slice the onions and large carrots and add them to the pan along with the cloves of garlic. Roast in the middle level of the oven for about 2½ hours or until the meat registers 165°F on a meat thermometer. (If you prefer an internal temperature of 185°F, continue roasting the pork, but it will have less juice and generally be drier.) While the pork is cooking, scrub, but do not peel, the baby carrots and radishes. Boil them in water for about 4 minutes or just until they begin to soften. Do not fully cook. Drain, transfer to a bowl and set aside. When the pork roast is done, remove it from the oven and let it sit for 15 minutes.

In a large frying pan, add the butter or olive oil and sauté the radishes and carrots. Add salt and white pepper to taste and about 1–2 teaspoons sugar. Toss the vegetables in the pan until they are slightly brown and the sugar has caramelized. Depending on the amount of residual pork fat in the roasting pan or your tolerance for it, you can add the radishes and carrots to the pan, or transfer the pork and some of its juices to a serving platter and surround the pork with the radishes and carrots.

*The meat should have as much fat on it as possible (a 4-pound pork shoulder will serve about six people).

†If baby carrots are not available, substitute 1 cup of julienned carrots.

††French Breakfast radishes, which are white and pink-colored, are longer, thinner and milder than the round red radishes usually found in the US. If you use red radishes, quarter them.

Seiche aux Poireaux

Cuttlefish sautéed with leeks. Serves 4.

This recipe comes from Jean Vaché, of Clapiers, near Montpellier. He learned it from his mother but the dish has been in their family for several generations. Cuttlefish is a cephalopod, not a fish. It typically is not found in North American waters. We have substituted squid, a close relative, which is delicious, relatively inexpensive, and, as yet, plentiful.

> 2 POUNDS LEEKS
>
> 5 SCALLIONS
>
> 4 TABLESPOONS OLIVE OIL
>
> 2 POUNDS SQUID, CUT LENGTHWISE INTO STRIPS ¼–½ INCHES WIDE
>
> ½ CUP DRY WHITE WINE OR VERMOUTH
>
> SEVERAL SPRIGS OF FRESH THYME AND ROSEMARY
>
> ½ TEASPOON SALT OR TO TASTE
>
> FRESHLY GROUND BLACK PEPPER

Wash and clean the leeks. Thinly slice the leeks and scallions, including the white parts and a small amount of the more-tender green parts. Sauté the vegetables in 2 tablespoons olive oil over medium heat until they are translucent and slightly soft, about 3–5 minutes. Set aside. In another frying pan, sauté the strips of squid in 2 tablespoons olive oil until they begin to soften, about 5 minutes. Strain the squid and add it to the pan with the leeks and scallions. Add the white wine, herbs, salt and pepper to taste. Cover and cook over low heat for about 2–3 minutes. Do not overcook, or the squid will be rubbery.

Brandade de Morue en Feuilleté

Cod in puff pastry crust. Serves 4.

This recipe is adapted from one prepared by chef Erick Vedel. Vedel, a native of Arles, has been teaching Provençal cuisine since 1995.

> 14 OUNCES OF SALT COD
>
> 2 LARGE CLOVES GARLIC
>
> JUICE OF HALF A LEMON
>
> 1 CUP RICOTTA-STYLE CHEESE (NOT FAT-FREE)
>
> 1–2 TABLESPOONS OLIVE OIL
>
> PINCH SALT
>
> PUFF PASTRY FOR EITHER ONE 12-INCH CIRCLE, OR TWO 8-INCH CIRCLES
>
> ONE EGG YOLK PLUS 1 TEASPOON WATER FOR EGG WASH

Soak the salt cod in water for 24 hours (refrigerated), changing the water once or twice. Bring a large pot of water, enough to cover the cod by an inch, to a gentle boil and poach the fish for about 4 minutes. Drain and set aside.

Peel and mash the garlic until smooth. Combine the garlic and lemon juice into a paste. Flake the salt cod into fine pieces. (If the cod has skin and bones, remove them first.) If you have a large mortar and pestle, crush the fish in it. If not, you can use a food processor, processing for just a few seconds until the fish begins to break down. You want to crush the cod not purée it. It should look like crabmeat not mashed potatoes. Transfer to a large bowl.

Mix the ricotta and cod together. Add the olive oil and salt to taste. Whip in the garlic and lemon juice with a fork. The *brandade* can be set aside at this point and kept until you are ready to prepare the puff pastry.

If you are using commercial puff pastry, defrost it in the refrigerator a few hours before use, or follow the manufacturer's instructions. Roll out the dough to form one 12" circle or two 8" circles, ⅛" thick. Fill the lower half of the circle with the *brandade*, keeping a 1" border along the edge. Use a knife or spatula to evenly distribute the *brandade*. Fold the top half of the puff pastry over the filling to form a

[Brandade de Morue en Feuilleté, *continued*]
pocket. Seal or crimp the edges. Score the top of the pastry lightly with a knife in a crosshatch pattern. Paint the top of the puff pastry with egg wash.

Preheat the oven to 350°F. Bake the *brandade* for about 30 minutes or until the dough is puffy and golden. Serve immediately.

Excess *brandade* mixture is delicious spread on slices of toasted French bread, or mixed with mashed potatoes.

Aiguillettes de Poulet Panées au Pain d'Épices

Fried chicken cutlets with a gingerbread crust. Serves 4.

This recipe was contributed by Catherine Petitjean-Dugourd, CEO of the Mulot & Petitjean company in Dijon, founded in 1796 and family-owned and operated for generations. Spice cake (loosely translated as gingerbread) has been a specialty of the city for centuries. Madame Petitjean-Dugourd recommends serving this dish with rice and chutney. Although these accompaniments do not sound particularly French, their use shows the continuing influence of the spice trade, and things exotic, on France.

> 4 SKINLESS, BONELESS CHICKEN CUTLETS (ABOUT 1½ POUNDS)
>
> SALT AND PEPPER TO TASTE
>
> FLOUR FOR DREDGING (ABOUT 1 CUP)
>
> 2 EGGS, BEATEN
>
> ¾ CUP DRIED GINGERBREAD CRUMBS OR GROUND GINGER SNAP COOKIES
>
> 2–4 TABLESPOONS CANOLA OIL

The chicken cutlets should be ¼–½" thick. If they are thicker, place them between sheets of plastic wrap and pound with a mallet. If cutlets are unavailable, use breasts, and cut or pound them to the appropriate thickness. Pat the chicken dry with paper towels. Salt and pepper to taste. Dredge the cutlets in flour, dip them in beaten eggs, and then roll them in the gingerbread or ginger snap cookie crumbs. Heat 2 tablespoons of canola oil in a large frying pan and fry the cutlets over medium to high heat, turning them as they brown. You may have to do this in two batches. Reduce the heat to medium until the cutlets are cooked through, about 10 minutes. Drain on paper towels. Serve.

Carré d'Agneau en Croûte d'Herbes

Rack of lamb in an herb crust. Serves 4.

This recipe comes from Brigitte Tilleray, author of several cookbooks including *The Frenchwoman's Kitchen*. Tilleray lives in an area of Normandy where *agneau de pré-salé,* lamb raised along the coastal salt marshes, is a specialty. This is one of Tilleray's favorite dishes, especially in spring and summer when she says the meat is at its best. Ask your butcher to prepare the lamb, making sure that the backbone has been removed. The lamb can be frenched, with the meat and fat connecting the rib bones removed, or cap-off, leaving more of the meat on. Either way, this is a luxurious piece of meat, perfect for celebrations. Serve with boiled new potatoes and green peas.

For the lamb

8 SPRIGS PARSLEY

8 SPRIGS CHERVIL

1 SPRIG FRESH ROSEMARY

3 SPRIGS FRESH THYME

3 FRESH MINT LEAVES

2 GARLIC CLOVES, PEELED

4 SLICES GOOD-QUALITY WHITE BREAD, CRUSTS REMOVED

1 TABLESPOON FRENCH MUSTARD OR WORCESTERSHIRE SAUCE

ABOUT 7 TABLESPOONS OLIVE OIL

8 LOIN CHOPS IN ONE PIECE OR RACK, EXCESS FAT REMOVED*

For the vegetables

1 POUND SMALL NEW POTATOES

2 TABLESPOONS BUTTER

1 CUP WATER

3–4 OUTER LEAVES OF A LETTUCE

3 SCALLIONS

BOUQUET GARNI OF THYME, PARSLEY AND BAY LEAF

1 POUND FRESH OR FROZEN PEAS

1–2 TABLESPOONS FINELY CHOPPED MINT

SALT AND PEPPER TO TASTE

Preheat the oven to 475°F. Remove the herbs from their stems and process them in a food processor along with the garlic and bread. Add the mustard or Worcestershire sauce and about 5 tablespoons of olive oil, 1 tablespoon at a time, and continue processing until a thick paste forms. (The amount of oil needed will depend on the volume of herbs.) Rub the lamb with 2 tablespoons of olive oil and spread the herb paste generously over the meat.

Roast the meat for 15 minutes at 475°F, then lower the heat to 400°F and cook for another 30 minutes. Turn the oven off and cover the meat with thick aluminum foil. Leave the meat in the oven with the oven door open for another 10 minutes. (The French typically eat lamb that is cooked pink. For more well-done meat, add about 15 minutes to the cooking time at 400°F.)

[Carré d'Agneau en Croûte d'Herbes, *continued*]

While the lamb is cooking, place the new potatoes with their skins on in a pot of water and boil until they are soft when pierced with a sharp knife. When ready to serve, drain the potatoes and return them to the heat to remove any remaining liquid. Add 1 tablespoon of butter and toss the potatoes.

Wash the lettuce leaves. Chop the white parts and some of the green stalks of the scallions. Put water, 1 tablespoon of butter, the lettuce, scallions and bouquet garni in a saucepan and bring to a boil over high heat. Reduce the heat to a simmer, add the peas and cook, covered, for 2–3 minutes until the peas are tender, adding more water if necessary. Remove the bouquet garni.

To serve, place the rack of lamb on a platter surrounded by the potatoes and peas. Sprinkle the potatoes with chopped mint and salt and pepper to taste.

*If rack of lamb is not available, substitute single lamb chops.

Vegetables and Salads

Tourte de Carottes en Robe de Chou
Carrot and cabbage bake. Serves 6–8.

This recipe comes from Brigitte Tilleray, author of several books on travel and cooking, including *The Frenchwoman's Kitchen*. Tilleray hails from Normandy, where carrots, cabbage and leeks are the foundation for many of the region's stews and soups. Tilleray says this dish is ideal for accompanying poultry and pork dishes but can be served on its own as a vegetarian dish, along with a cream and chive sauce.

Carrot and cabbage bake

8 LARGE CABBAGE LEAVES

4 LARGE CARROTS, PEELED AND TRIMMED

3 MEDIUM TURNIPS, PEELED

3 MEDIUM ONIONS

1 SMALL BUNCH OF PARSLEY, STEMS REMOVED

3 YOUNG LEEKS, CLEANED, WHITE PARTS ONLY

½ CUP UNSALTED BUTTER

1 SMALL CLOVE GARLIC

1 TEASPOON SALT OR TO TASTE

½ TEASPOON WHITE PEPPER

3 LARGE EGGS, BEATEN

2–4 ADDITIONAL TABLESPOONS BUTTER

Sauce (optional)

2 TABLESPOONS BUTTER

½ CUP CRÈME FRAÎCHE

SALT AND PEPPER TO TASTE

2 TEASPOONS CHOPPED CHIVES

Carefully wash the cabbage leaves and blanch them a few at a time in a large (4-quart) saucepan or Dutch oven filled with boiling salted water. Transfer them to a large bowl of very cold water, or cool them under the tap. Lay them out on kitchen towels and pat dry. Grate the carrots and turnips, or process them in a food processor until grated fine. Chop the onions, parsley and leeks.

In a heavy saucepan, melt the stick of butter. Add all the vegetables and herbs except the cabbage, and sweat them over medium to low heat for 15 minutes, stirring occasionally. Season with salt and pepper. Set aside to cool for a few minutes, then add the beaten eggs.

Preheat the oven to 375°F. Butter an 8" round baking dish or cake pan. Line it with the cabbage leaves, overlapping the edge of the dish. Reserve one or two leaves for the top. Spoon the vegetable and egg mixture into the pan, covering the top with the reserved cabbage leaves. Dot the top of the cabbage with a few small pieces of butter. Cover the dish loosely with aluminum foil and bake for about 20 minutes or until the mixture is set and a skewer inserted into the middle comes out clean.

To make the sauce, melt the butter and crème fraîche over low heat, add the chives and season to taste.

To serve, run a knife around the edges of the carrot and cabbage bake and place a platter over the dish. Invert the platter and dish together and give them a good shake to release onto the platter. Serve the sauce alongside the dish.

Gratin Dauphinois
Scalloped potatoes. Serves 6–8.

This dish, shared by Colette Manin, takes its name from the Dauphiné, a once-independent region that became attached to France in 1349 on the condition that the heir apparent to the throne hold the title of Dauphin. It is a classic dish and should be part of any cook's repertoire. Note that it uses cream, not cheese.

1–2 TABLESPOONS OLIVE OIL

2 CUPS CRÈME FRAÎCHE

¾ CUP 2% MILK

2 CLOVES GARLIC, FINELY CHOPPED

2–2½ POUNDS POTATOES, PEELED, AND SLICED (⅛-INCH THICK)

SALT AND FRESHLY GROUND PEPPER TO TASTE

[Gratin Dauphinois, *continued*]

Preheat oven to 400°F. Grease the bottom and sides of a 9 × 14" baking dish with the olive oil. In a bowl, whisk the crème fraîche and milk until the milk is thoroughly incorporated and the mixture is smooth. Spread the garlic on the bottom of the baking dish. Place a layer of potatoes on top of the garlic. Sprinkle with salt and pepper. Spread a scant cup of the milk-and-cream mixture on top of the potatoes. The potatoes should not be completely covered. Repeat twice more. Place the dish in the middle level of the oven and bake for about 45 minutes or until the potatoes are golden and bubbly.

Tian de Courgettes et de Tomates

Zucchini and tomato casserole. Serves 4.

This recipes comes from Erick Vedel, who operates a cooking school in Arles, in Provence. The *tian* takes its name from the casserole dish in which it typically is served. The key in preparing the dish is not to crowd the vegetables, but to let them cook so that the olive oil and vegetable juices combine.

> 1 MEDIUM SWEET ONION, COARSELY CHOPPED
>
> 6–10 TABLESPOONS OLIVE OIL
>
> 5 MEDIUM TOMATOES, QUARTERED
>
> 2–3 BAY LEAVES
>
> 2 MEDIUM ZUCCHINI, SLICED IN HALF LENGTHWISE AND COARSELY CHOPPED
>
> SEA SALT

In a large, non-stick pan over medium-high heat, sweat the chopped onion in 3–5 tablespoons olive oil until translucent, about 5 minutes. (Do not stint on the olive oil.) Add tomatoes and bay leaves. Cook over medium heat until the tomatoes are soft but not mushy and most of the liquid is absorbed. While the tomatoes cook, sauté the zucchini in 3–5 tablespoons of olive oil in a second large, non-stick pan until completely brown on all sides. Remove with a slotted spoon and set aside. When ready to serve, combine the tomatoes and zucchini in a *tian,* or earthenware casserole dish. Sprinkle lightly with sea salt.

DESSERTS

Tarte aux Chocolat et Bananes Sonia Rykiel

Sonia Rykiel chocolate and banana tart. Serves 4–8.

This recipe comes from master chocolatier Christian Constant. Constant, whose chocolate and pastry shop is on Paris's rue d'Assas near the Jardins du Luxembourg, believes chocolate is much like wine, with powerful subtleties from region to region. He named this delectable tart after French fashion designer Sonia Rykiel.

An 8" straight-sided tart ring or fluted tart mold with removable bottom is needed to make this dessert.

Crust

1½ CUPS ALL-PURPOSE FLOUR

7 TABLESPOONS UNSALTED BUTTER, SOFTENED

¾ CUP CONFECTIONERS' SUGAR

PINCH OF SALT

1 LARGE EGG, BEATEN

Filling

½ CUP HEAVY (WHIPPING) CREAM

5½ OUNCES OF BEST-QUALITY BITTERSWEET CHOCOLATE

1 TABLESPOON UNSALTED BUTTER, SOFTENED

4 PERFECT BANANAS, JUST ON THE EDGE OF RIPENESS

¼ CUP APRICOT OR PEACH JAM

A FEW DROPS OF RUM (OPTIONAL)

To make the crust, combine the flour and softened butter (by hand or in a food processor) until it has the consistency of cornmeal. Add the confectioners' sugar, salt and egg. Mix or process just until the dough combines. It should be smooth and satiny. (An alternate and equally effective technique starts with combining the sugar and butter in a mixer, adding the egg and salt, then, finally, the flour.) Wrap in waxed paper and refrigerate for several hours or overnight.

When you are ready to roll out the dough, let it soften at room temperature for about 5 minutes. Place the tart ring or mold on a silicon baking mat or a cookie sheet lined with parchment paper. Roll the dough out on a lightly floured surface to form an 8" circle, about ¼" thick. Drape the dough over a floured rolling pin and lift it into the tart mold or ring. The dough is forgiving; if you need to start over, re-form it into a ball, chill it for a few minutes and start again. Cut off any dough hanging over the edge of the pan. It can be used to repair breaks in the shell. Prick the dough on the bottom—not the sides—with a fork. Refrigerate for a few minutes (or freeze).

Bake the tart in a preheated 400°F oven. The tart is done when it begins to turn golden. Do not over bake. Cool the tart on a rack and remove the ring when it is completely cool. If you are using a tart pan, remove the tart from the mold carefully by pushing up from the bottom and releasing the sides. Then, using a long spatula or the base of another tart mold, remove the bottom. Keep the tart shell in a cool, dry place until ready to use (but not for more than a day).

To prepare the filling, cut the chocolate into small pieces and place them in a glass or ceramic bowl. Set aside. Heat the cream in a small pan over medium heat until it almost comes to a boil, and pour it on top of the chocolate. Stir the chocolate gently

[Tarte aux Chocolat et Bananes Sonia Rykiel, *continued*]
until it is completely melted. Add the softened butter and stir. (If the chocolate or butter hasn't completely melted, microwave the chocolate for a few seconds at a time, no more than 10, at half power. Or gently warm the chocolate in the top of a double boiler.) Let the warm chocolate settle for a few minutes, until it begins to thicken. Pour it immediately into the cooled tart shell.

Peel and cut the bananas into ¼" slices. Carefully overlap the slices in a circle, beginning from the outside edge. Begin the second row with the bananas facing in the opposite direction. In the center, place up-ended or diced banana slices.

To glaze the tart, heat the jam in a small pan until it becomes liquid. Press the jam through a very fine strainer to eliminate any solids. If you like, you can add a few drops of rum. Paint the bananas and the rim of the tart with the glaze. Keep the tart in a cool place (where the chocolate will not melt) until ready to serve.

Cocotte de Fruits au Vin Épicé avec Diablotins aux Amandes

Fruits poached in mulled wine with almond cakes. Serves 4.

This recipe is adapted from one provided by Didier Robert, chef of Le Piano Qui Fume, a small neighborhood restaurant in Dijon. Chef Robert, who worked in Michelin-starred restaurants across France, was born and raised in Burgundy. This dessert is a dish that is good for all seasons, using different kinds of fruit, both fresh—at the top of their flavor—and dried. Although Chef Robert serves the dish with little cakes and ice cream, that may be gilding the lily. The dish stands beautifully on its own. (See photo on front cover.)

Fruit and wine

1⅔ CUPS FULL-BODIED RED WINE, SUCH AS MERLOT

¼ CUP SUGAR

1-INCH PIECE LEMON ZEST

1-INCH PIECE ORANGE ZEST

½ STICK OF CINNAMON

¼ VANILLA BEAN, CUT IN HALF LENGTHWISE

1 STAR ANISE

2 CUPS FRESH OR DRIED FRUIT, IN BITE-SIZED PIECES

VANILLA ICE CREAM (OPTIONAL)

Almond cakes

SCANT ¼ CUP ALMONDS, GROUND FINE

¼ CUP CONFECTIONERS' SUGAR

2 TABLESPOONS BUTTER, SOFTENED

3 TABLESPOONS ALL-PURPOSE FLOUR

YOLK OF 1 EGG

A FEW PIECES OF SLICED ALMONDS

1½ TEASPOONS OF RUM

2 SLICES OF CAKE, SUCH AS SPICE CAKE* OR POUND CAKE

The night before you intend to serve the dish, bring the wine to a boil in a medium saucepan and flambé it. (Use a long match as a precaution.) Add the sugar, zests, vanilla bean and spices. Simmer for 10 minutes. Add the fruits in order of ripeness. Apples and firm pears will take about 10 minutes, raspberries and strawberries a few seconds. Once the fruit is cooked, remove the pan from the heat and let the wine and fruit juices combine. Refrigerate until ready to use. (The fruits can be served at room temperature or gently heated until warm.)

Make the almond paste by grinding the almonds in a food processor. Add the sugar, butter, flour, egg yolk and rum. The paste should be thick enough to spread on the cake. (The almond paste can be refrigerated, then softened when ready to use.)

Using a knife or cookie cutter, cut the slices of cake into shapes or pieces about 2" across. Spread a small amount of almond paste on each piece. Place a few slices of almond on top and bake in a 350°F oven for about 15 minutes or until browned.

To assemble, place the fruit in *cocottes* or small serving dishes, or on dessert plates. Place the cake alongside the fruit. Serve with a scoop of vanilla ice cream, if desired.

*See p. 64 for a recipe for *pain d'épices* (spice cake).

Tarte Tatin aux Abricots

Caramelized upside-down fruit tart with apricots. Serves 4.

This recipe from Provençal chef Erick Vedel is a variation on the French bistro classic (see *Menu Guide,* p. 102), using olive oil instead of butter, and apricots instead of apples. When Vedel showed me how to make the dish, he used apples and bananas, but pears, peaches or nectarines are good, too, no matter what purists and the Brotherhood (*Confrérie*) of the *Tarte Tatin* say. The fruit should be firm enough to stand up to both stovetop and oven cooking. Vedel also used puff pastry instead of *pâte brisée,* or flaky pastry, but either one works.

1 TABLESPOON OLIVE OIL

8 SMALL TO MEDIUM FRESH APRICOTS*

¼ CUP SUGAR

ONE 9-INCH FLAKY PIE CRUST (SEE RECIPE, P. 68) OR PUFF PASTRY

CONFECTIONERS' SUGAR (OPTIONAL)

On a floured surface, roll out a circle of dough approximately 9" in diameter and ¼" thick. Put the dough, covered, on a sheet of waxed paper and refrigerate until ready to use.

[Tarte Tatin aux Abricots, *continued*]

Preheat oven to 325°F. In a 9" non-stick ovenproof frying pan, heat the olive oil and swirl until the oil covers the entire pan. Shake or sift the sugar over the olive oil, covering the oil completely. Cut the apricots in half and place them cut-side down in circles in the pan. Cook over medium to low heat, gently shaking the pan occasionally, until the sugar caramelizes and the apricots begin to soft, about 10 minutes. Take care not to burn the sugar.

When the apricots are soft, remove the pan from the stove. Working quickly, remove the circle of dough from the refrigerator and place it loosely on top of the apricots, making sure it does not extend beyond the pan. Bake the tart in the oven for about 20 minutes or until the crust is golden brown. Remove from the oven and immediately invert a heat-resistant plate (at least an inch wider than the frying pan and preferably with a slight lip) over the frying pan and flip the tart into the plate, being careful not to spill the hot, caramelized liquid. Rearrange any fruit that may have slipped out of place. Serve hot, either plain, dusted with confectioners' sugar, or with vanilla ice cream.

*Apples should be firm varieties, such as Granny Smiths, Fujis or Golden Delicious. Peel, core and quarter them. Bananas should be firm and cut in half lengthwise. If mixing fruit, make sure the fruit is at the same height.

Pain d'Épices

Spice cake. Serves many.

This recipe is adapted from one provided by Colette Robert, mother of Le Piano Qui Fume's chef, Didier Robert, in Dijon. *Pain d'épices* is one of the most popular cakes in Burgundy, found routinely on restaurant menus and sold in stores. *Pain d'épices* is not just a sweet but accompanies meat and poultry dishes.

> 1 TEASPOON BUTTER TO GREASE THE PAN
>
> ½ CUP MILK
>
> ¼ CUP PLUS 1 TABLESPOON HONEY
>
> 3 TABLESPOONS BUTTER, SOFTENED
>
> 2½ OUNCES OR A SCANT ½ CUP PACKED DARK BROWN SUGAR
>
> 1 CUP PLUS 1 TABLESPOON ALL-PURPOSE FLOUR
>
> 1½ TEASPOONS BAKING POWDER
>
> 1 TEASPOON ALLSPICE
>
> 1 TEASPOON POWDERED ANISE
>
> 1 LARGE EGG, BEATEN

Preheat oven to 350°F. Butter an 8 × 4" loaf pan. Set aside. In a small saucepan, scald (but do not boil) the milk, then remove it from the stove. Add the honey, butter and sugar, stirring until the butter has melted and all the ingredients are incorporated. In a bowl, sift the flour, baking powder and spices. Fold in the milk mixture. Add the beaten egg and stir until the mixture is smooth. Pour the batter into the loaf pan and bake at 350°F for 25 minutes. Reduce the oven temperature to 300°F and bake for another 10–15 minutes, or until a toothpick inserted in the middle of the cake comes out clean.

La Pogne

Sweet cake. Serves 6.

Pogne, made from a brioche-type dough and formed in the shape of a crown, is a specialty of the region around Lyon and Valence. This recipe is adapted from one shared by Joëlle Manin, who in turn had adapted it from that of an elderly neighbor in Bourg-de-Péage, northeast of Valence.

> 1 OUNCE OF CAKE YEAST
>
> PINCH OF SUGAR
>
> ¼ CUP WARM WATER
>
> 3 LARGE EGGS, BEATEN
>
> ½ CUP BUTTER, MELTED AND COOLED
>
> 1 TABLESPOON ORANGE WATER
>
> 1 TABLESPOON RUM
>
> ZEST OF A SMALL ORANGE
>
> ZEST OF A SMALL LEMON
>
> 3½ CUPS CAKE FLOUR
>
> PINCH OF SALT
>
> ¾ CUP SUGAR
>
> 1 EGG YOLK
>
> 1 TEASPOON WATER

Proof the yeast with a pinch of sugar in about ¼ cup of warm but not hot water, about 5 minutes. (Do not proof in a metal bowl.) Place the beaten eggs, butter, orange water, rum and citrus zests in the bowl of an electric mixer. Mix until the liquids just come together. Gently add the proofed yeast.

Mix together the flour, salt, and sugar. Add them to the mixing bowl. Using a dough hook, knead for about 15 minutes. Add a little more flour if necessary. The dough should be smooth and elastic. Remove the dough from the mixer with a spatula or rubber spoon and place it in a bowl dusted with flour. Cover and let rise in a warm place for several hours or overnight. The dough should more than double in size. Push the dough down, knead it gently for a few seconds and place it on a baking sheet lined with parchment paper. Use a 2"-diameter cookie ring or glass to create a hole in the middle of the dough. Leave the mold in the dough to hold it in place

[La Pogne, *continued*]

while it rises again until about double in size, about 2 hours.
Preheat oven to 325°F. Mix the egg yolk with a teaspoon of water to create an egg wash. Remove the glass or cookie ring from the *pogne*. Brush the egg wash over the *pogne* and, using a sharp knife, make a few gashes lengthwise down the sides of the dough. Bake the *pogne* at 325°F for 15 minutes, then increase the temperature to 350°F and bake for an additional 20–30 minutes until the *pogne* looks golden brown and sounds hollow when you tap it with your finger. Serve warm or at room temperature.

Teurgoule

Rice pudding. Serves 8.

This recipe was inspired by Lionel Varin, a *pâtissier* and pastry teacher, now retired, and his wife, Marie-France, of Hauville, near Rouen; and by the *Confrérie des Gastronomes de la Teurgoule et de la Fallue de Normandie,* an organization that celebrates *teurgoule* and another traditional regional dish, *la fallue,* by regularly sponsoring a cooking contest. *Teurgoule,* a very thick rice pudding, and *fallue,* a dry cake, are often served together at the end of a celebration, such as a wedding. There are many variations of *teurgoule,* but the Varins are purists. They insist that only the basic ingredients should be included—no eggs, butter, flavorings (such as vanilla extract) or raisins.

> 8 CUPS (HALF A GALLON) OF WHOLE OR 2% MILK
>
> ¾ CUP ROUND OR ARBORIO-STYLE RICE
>
> 1 CUP FIRMLY PACKED BROWN SUGAR
>
> 2 TEASPOONS CINNAMON
>
> PINCH OF SALT

Preheat oven to 350°F. Wash the rice, then blanch it in a small saucepan for 4 minutes in rapidly boiling water to cover. Remove the rice from the heat and strain. Place the rice in a 4-quart, oven-safe mixing bowl, along with the sugar, salt and cinnamon. Stir in the milk. Bake the *teurgoule* for 30 minutes at 350°F, reduce the oven temperature to 300°F, and bake for 5 hours. The *teurgoule* will develop a brownish crust (from the sugar and cinnamon) and seem slightly runny, but the milk and rice will harden as it cools. Serve at room temperature.

MISCELLANEOUS

Vinaigrette Façon Bridget Pugh

Bridget Pugh's vinaigrette.

This vinaigrette accompanies chef Bridget Pugh's fillet of sea bass, on p. 49. But it is equally good with a plain garden salad.

A FEW PIECES OF FRESH FENNEL TOPS

JUICE OF 1 LEMON

1 TABLESPOON PASTIS (ANISE-FLAVORED LIQUEUR)

1 CUP TOP-QUALITY OLIVE OIL

½ TEASPOON SUGAR

½ TEASPOON SEA SALT

In a blender, process the fennel for a few seconds, then add the remaining ingredients and blend until the mixture thickens. Refrigerate until ready to use. Vinaigrette can be stored for several days.

Pâte à Pizza
Pizza dough.

This recipe is adapted from Saulieu chef Patrick Auduc's. Pizza is not on his restaurant's menu, but is eaten in the kitchen by the family, before the restaurant opens for dinner. When I watched him prepare the pizza, Auduc began by rolling out the dough, spreading on tomato sauce, then adding slices of sausage, canned snails, parsley, grated cheese and a few pats of butter. He baked it in a 400°F oven until the crust was browned and the cheese melted, about 20 minutes. You can use your own topping or try chef Peter Shaw's recipe for *Tarte de Tomates et Poivrons Rouges* on p. 46.

1 TABLESPOON YEAST

PINCH OF SUGAR

2 TABLESPOONS WARM WATER

2 CUPS ALL-PURPOSE FLOUR

⅛ CUP OLIVE OIL

ABOUT ¾ CUP WATER

ABOUT 1 TABLESPOON OLIVE OIL

Proof the yeast and sugar in the water for about 5 minutes, letting the mixture foam. Put the flour in a mixing bowl or food processor, then add the yeast, olive oil and just enough water for the mixture to form into a ball. Knead the dough for a few minutes (adding more flour if necessary) until it becomes soft and satiny. Lightly grease a clean mixing bowl with the tablespoon of olive oil and place the dough in the bowl. Cover with a damp cloth and let rise until doubled in bulk. (One good way of doing this is to set the bowl inside a gas oven with the pilot light on.) When the dough has risen, punch it down and roll it out to fit an 8½ × 12" pan or free-form it on a pizza pan. Add the desired topping and bake at 400°F until the crust is brown and the topping is heated through, about 20 minutes.

Pâte Brisée

Flaky pie crust. Makes one 9-inch pie crust.

> 1½ CUPS ALL-PURPOSE FLOUR
>
> PINCH OF SALT
>
> ¼ CUP SUGAR (OMIT FOR SAVORY PIE)
>
> ¾ CUP CHILLED, UNSALTED BUTTER, CUT INTO SMALL PIECES
>
> 1 LARGE EGG
>
> ABOUT 4 TABLESPOONS ICED WATER

Place flour, salt and sugar in a food processor. Pulse for a few seconds to mix the ingredients together. Cut the butter into small pieces, add to the processor and pulse for about 5–10 seconds or until the mixture resembles coarse meal. Beat the egg and add to the mixture, again pulsing for a few seconds. Add a few tablespoons of iced water, about 2 at a time just until the dough begins to come together. Gather the dough into a ball and wrap in wax paper. Chill for at least 30 minutes before rolling out.

Le For' Bon Tartine

The really good sandwich. Serves 1.
This sandwich is served at the Cuisine de Bar, next door to the Poilâne bakery, on Paris's rue du Cherche-Midi. The open-faced sandwich is a hearty riff on *croque-Monsieur,* the bistro classic.

> 1 SLICE SOURDOUGH BREAD, ABOUT 7 INCHES LONG AND ¼-INCH THICK
>
> 1 SAINT-MARCELLIN CHEESE, ABOUT 3 OUNCES*
>
> 2 THIN SLICES BAYONNE HAM
>
> 1–2 TABLESPOONS OLIVE OIL
>
> CHIVES, SNIPPED

Place the bread on a baking sheet. Cut the Saint-Marcellin cheese in half or quarters and place across the bread. Top with the ham slices. Grill the sandwich in a toaster oven or under the broiler for a few minutes until the cheese begins to melt and the ham crisps. Remove from the oven and drizzle with olive oil. Top with snipped chives. Serve with a green salad and small bowls of condiments including sea salt, cumin seeds and dried oregano.
*Brie or a fresh goat's-milk cheese may be substituted.

Shopping in France's Food Markets

Helpful Tips

Outdoor Markets

Wherever you go in France, whatever the season or day of the week, you will find an outdoor market (*marché*) offering a wealth of products. Although the French also shop in corner grocery stores, supermarkets and all-purpose hypermarkets or superstores that sell virtually everything, the tradition of shopping at a neighborhood outdoor market remains strong.

Markets are the perfect place to learn about regional delicacies and culinary traditions, and to converse with French men and women engaged in something they are always passionate about—food.

As with most markets, whatever the country, some general rules apply. The sellers are there to do business. While they're happy to discuss their products—how they're grown or prepared, what's in them—and offer you a sample, the merchants would be delighted if you made a purchase, even if it's quite small. They are also glad to oblige the photographer, but it is common courtesy to ask permission first.

Indoor or Fixed Markets

Covered markets are worth seeking out, if just for the architecture alone. Some are housed in magnificent halls (*halles*) built at the turn of the 20th century and made of cast iron, brick and glass. Unlike outdoor markets, which are open two or three days a week, covered markets may operate more frequently and keep longer hours. There are also permanent shops located along pedestrian malls or market streets that are especially attractive shopping centers when the stores move out-of-doors with displays.

Specialty Markets

There are several specialty markets, for example those selling organic products (*produits biologiques*). The grandfather of all wholesale markets is Rungis, just outside of Paris. The market was established in 1969 with the closing of the central city market, Les Halles, a fixture of Parisian life and commerce for centuries. Only wholesalers can shop at Rungis, but visitors can certainly watch the action. See also www.rungisinternational.com.

Weights, Measures and International Regulations

The French use the metric system. Products will be priced in euros, by the kilogram, the equivalent of 2.2 pounds. The following abbreviated list of approximate weights is usually enough to get the desired quantities:

> *Cent grammes*: 100 grams (¹⁄₁₀ kilo), or about ¼ pound
> *Deux cent cinquante grammes*: 250 grams (¼ kilo), or about ½ pound
> *Cinq cent grammes*: 500 grams (½ kilo), or about 1 pound

If you are considering bringing food back to the United States, check the website of the US Customs and Border Protection beforehand to see which items or categories of items you are allowed to bring into the country. Go to www.cbp.gov and click on "Travel."

A Health Precaution

Wherever you travel it is wise to choose your food vendors with care, following the same criteria you would use at home. Don't ask for trouble. Eating unclean produce can result in transmission of unpleasant ailments or serious illnesses. Make sure produce looks fresh and clean. Should you have any doubts, look for stalls that appear popular with local people. Bottled water is readily available everywhere. It is a good thing to have on hand for drinking and for washing fruits and vegetables. Also be advised that eating raw or undercooked foods may increase the risk of food-borne illness.

Resources

Online Suppliers of French Food Items

In the US, French products or ingredients, such as mustards, pickles, honey, olive oils, vinegars, sea salt, lentils, canned vegetables and pâtés, can be found in many specialty stores and, increasingly, neighborhood supermarkets. Local farmers' markets are also good sources for the building blocks of the best French dishes—fresh fruits and vegetables, farm-raised meats and poultry, including rabbit, and artisanal breads and cheeses. You can often find close approximations and sometimes the real thing, such as locally grown French melons, green beans (*haricots verts*), white asparagus, fingerling potatoes, frisée lettuce and French Breakfast radishes. There are many online suppliers of French food items in the US and some in France that ship to the US. These can be especially helpful when looking for a particular brand or hard-to-find products, such as chestnut honey from the Pyrenees and rendered duck fat. A few companies are listed below.

For a wide range of French gourmet and grocery items, and miscellaneous kitchen and household items, such as soaps, tableware and linens:

Joie de Vivre
Tel 800-648-8854
info@frenchselections.com
www.frenchselections.com

Saveur du Jour
Tel 408-844-4155
info@saveurdujour.com
www.saveurdujour.com

The Frenchy Bee
Tel 866-379-9975
www.thefrenchybee.com

Le Village
Tel 888-873-7194
www.levillage.com

For French and other international gourmet foods, including cheeses, meats, poultry, olive oils, vinegars, condiments or sweets:

igourmet.com
Tel 877-446-8763
www.igourmet.com

Gourmet-Food.com
Tel 770-485-0878
www.gourmet-food.com

Gourmet Food Store
Tel 877-220-4181
www.gourmetfoodstore.com

Oliviers & Company
Tel 877-828-6620
www.oliviersandco.com

For specialized products:

D'Artagnan
Tel 800-327-8246
orders@dartagnan.com
www.dartagnan.com
(foie gras, organic poultry, meats)

L'Epicerie
Tel 866-350-7575
www.lepicerie.com
(molecular gastronomy)

Mirepoix USA
Tel 510-590-6693
info@foiegras.com
www.enjoyfoiegras.com
(foie gras, *charcuterie*)

Fromage.com
www.fromages.com
(France-based cheese firm)

For American importers of Poilâne products, contact the company in Paris.
Tel (011) (33) 1 45 48 42 59, info@poilane.fr or www.poilane.fr

In Wisconsin, Nala's Fromagerie imports Poilâne bread.
Tel 920-347-0334
www.nalascheese.com

For special cookware items:

Bridge Kitchenware
Tel 973-287-6163
info@bridgekitchenware.com
www.bridgekitchenware.com

Sur La Table
Tel 800-243-0852
www.surlatable.com

Some Useful Organizations to Know About

French Government Offices

The Embassy of France
4101 Reservoir Road, NW
Washington, DC 20007
Tel 202-944-6000
info@ambafrance-us.org
www.ambafrance-us.org

French Government Tourist Office
info.us@franceguide.com
http://us.franceguide.com

Cultural Services of the French Embassy
972 Fifth Avenue
New York, NY 10075
Tel 212-439-1400
Fax 212-439-1401
www.frenchculture.org
Promotes French arts, literature and education.

International Organizations

Two non-profit, international travel organizations, The Friendship Force and Servas, promote good will and understanding among people of different cultures. These organizations share similar ideals but operate somewhat differently. Friendship Force members travel in groups to host countries. Both itinerary and travel arrangements are made by a member acting as exchange director. These trips combine stays with a host family and group travel within the host country. Servas members travel independently and make their own contacts with fellow members in other countries, choosing hosts with attributes of interest from membership rosters.

For more information about membership in these groups:

Friendship Force International	US SERVAS, Inc.
127 Peachtreet St., Suite 501	1125 16th St., Suite 201
Atlanta, GA 30303	Arcata, CA 95521
Tel 404-522-9490	Tel 707-825-1714
Fax 404-688-6148	info@usservas.org
http://thefriendshipforce.org	http://usservas.org

The Alliance Française is an international network of over 1,000 local, independently operated franchises, with a central office in Paris. The centers (more than 100 of them in the US) promote the French language and francophone culture through classes, lecture series, concerts and performing arts events.

Alliance Française
Tel 202-944-6353
federation@afusa.org
www.alliance-us.org
www.fondation-alliancefr.org

The international Slow Food movement, headquartered in Italy, is a non-profit, member-supported, eco-gastronomic organization founded in 1989 to counteract fast food, fast life, and the disappearance of local food traditions. There are several conviviums or local chapters across France sponsoring various activities. The chapters are listed on Slow Food France's Web pages.

Slow Food France
9 Place Alphonse Jourdain
31000 Toulouse
France
france@slowfood.fr
www.slowfood.fr

Helpful Phrases

For Use in Restaurants and Food Markets

In the Restaurant

The following phrases in French will assist you in ordering food, learning more about the dish you ordered, and determining which specialties of a locality are available. Each phrase is also written phonetically to help with pronunciation. In French, there is usually equal accent on syllables. You will discover that French people heartily encourage attempts to converse with them in their language. By all means, give it a try at every opportunity.

DO YOU HAVE A MENU, PLEASE?	Avez-vous une carte, s'il vous plaît? *Ah-vay-vooz oon kart, seel voo play?*
MAY I SEE THE MENU, PLEASE?	Puis-je voir la carte, s'il vous plaît? *Pweej vwar lah kart, seel voo play?*
WHAT DO YOU RECOMMEND TODAY?	Qu'est-ce que vous recommandez aujourd'hui? *Kess kuh voo ruh-koh-mawn-day oh-joor-dwee?*
DO YOU HAVE . . . HERE? (ADD AN ITEM FROM THE MENU GUIDE OR THE FOODS & FLAVORS GUIDE.)	Avez-vous . . . ici? *Ah-vay-voo . . . ee-see?*

75

Helpful Phrases

WHAT IS THE "SPECIAL" FOR TODAY, PLEASE?

Quel est le plat du jour, s'il vous plaît?
Kell ay luh plah doo joor, seel voo play?

DO YOU HAVE ANY REGIONAL DISHES?

Avez-vous des plats régionaux?
Ah-vay-voo day plah ray-jee-oh-noh?

IS THIS DISH SPICY?

Ce plat est-il épicé?
Suh plah, ay-teel ay-pee-say?

MAY I/WE ORDER . . . ?

Puis-je/Pouvons-nous commander . . . ?
Pweej/Poo-vawn-noo koh-mawn-day . . . ?

WHAT IS IN THIS DISH, PLEASE?

Qu'y a-t-il dans ce plat, s'il vous plaît?
Kee ah-teel dawn suh plah, seel voo play?

WHAT ARE THE SEASONINGS IN THIS DISH, PLEASE?

Quel est l'assaisonnement de ce plat, s'il vous plaît?
Kell eh lah-say-sohn-mawn duh suh plah, seel voo play?

THANK YOU VERY MUCH. IT IS DELICIOUS.

Merci beaucoup. C'est délicieux.
Mare-see boh-koo. Say day-lee-syuh.

76

In the Market

The following phrases will help you make purchases and learn more about unfamiliar produce, spices and herbs.

WHAT ARE THE REGIONAL FRUITS AND VEGETABLES?

Quels sont les fruits et légumes régionaux?

Kell sawn lay froo-ee eh lay-goom ray-jee-oh-noh?

WHAT IS THIS CALLED?

Qu'est-ce que c'est?

Kess kuh say?

DO YOU SELL . . . HERE? (ADD AN ITEM FROM THE *FOODS & FLAVORS GUIDE*.)

Vendez-vous . . . ici?

Vawn-day voo . . . ee-see?

MAY I TASTE THIS?

Puis-je goûter?

Pweej goo-tay?

WHERE CAN I BUY FRESH . . . ?

Où est-ce que je peux acheter du/de la . . . frais/fraîche?

Oo ess kuh juh puh ah-shuh-tay doo/duh la . . . fray/fresh?

HOW MUCH IS THIS PER KILO?

C'est combien le kilo?

Say kohm-bee-an luh kee-loh?

TWO HUNDRED FIFTY GRAMS (¼ KILO) OF THIS, PLEASE.

Deux cent cinquante grammes de ceci, s'il vous plaît.

Duh sawn saihn-cawhnt gram duh suh-see, seel voo play.

MAY I PHOTOGRAPH THIS, PLEASE?

Permettez-vous que je prenne une photo, s'il vous plaît?

Pair-may-tay-voo kuh juh prehn oon foh-toh, seel voo play?

HELPFUL PHRASES

Other Useful Phrases

Sometimes it helps to see in writing a word or phrase that is said to you in French, because certain letters sound distinctly different in French than in English. You may be familiar with the word and its English translation but less familiar with its pronunciation. The following phrase comes in handy if you want to see the word or phrase you are hearing.

PLEASE WRITE IT ON THIS PIECE OF PAPER.

Pouvez-vous, s'il vous plaît, noter ceci sur cette feuille?

Poo-vay-voo, seel voo play, noh-tay suh-see soor set fuh-yuh?

Interested in French cooking utensils?

WHERE CAN I BUY COOKING UTENSILS?

Où puis-je acheter des ustensiles de cuisine?

Ooh pweej ah-shuh-tay dayz ooh-stahn-seel duh kwee-zeen?

And, of course, the following phrases also are useful to know.

WHERE ARE THE RESTROOMS, PLEASE?

Où sont les toilettes, s'il vous plaît?

Ooh sawhn lay twah-let, seel voo play?

CHECK, PLEASE.

L'addition, s'il vous plaît.

Lah-dee-see-yon, seel voo play.

DO YOU ACCEPT CREDIT CARDS?

Acceptez-vous les cartes de crédit?

Ahk-sep-tay-voo lay kahrt duh cray-dee?

Menu Guide

This extensive alphabetical listing of menu items with English translations is a compilation of entries taken from dozens of menus and cookbooks. The idea is to make ordering food in France easier. The list includes typical French dishes as well as specialties characteristic of different regions across the country. Classic regional dishes that should not be missed are labeled "regional classic" in the margin next to the menu entry. Some noteworthy dishes popular throughout much of the country—also not to be missed—are labeled "national favorite." Comments on some of our favorite dishes also are included in the margin. French is the usual language on menus, although in some tourist areas English translations are available. Many French people speak English.

Although custom and tradition are changing fast in France—with many French people now resorting to eating on the run or at their desks instead of enjoying a leisurely lunch at home or in a restaurant—great attention is still paid to the importance of taking time to appreciate good food and especially good company. Dining out is an important activity in France. Traditional French cuisine is enjoyed in several types of establishments ranging from simple street corner cafés and animated bistros and brasseries, to the most elegant and expensive Michelin-starred restaurants.

Here are a few guidelines in distinguishing one food establishment from another. An *auberge* is a country inn serving food and drink. A *café* or *café-bar* (so-called because of the *barre de comptoir* or foot rest at the base of the serving counter) is open most of the day for drinks and light meals and snacks, but may also serve a respectable lunch. A *bistro* (also spelled *bistrot*) is usually a small, neighborhood restaurant, the name perhaps a corruption of the Russian *bystra,* meaning "hurry up," or derived from *bistouille,* a mixture of brandy and hot coffee. Once a beer hall, the *brasserie* was a novelty in 1870s Paris, brought to the city by Alsatians after the Franco-Prussian war but not without beer on tap and some of Alsace's dishes. Today a *brasserie,* often remarkable for its brass and chrome decor, serves standard French dishes. It is an especially good place for seafood. A *buffet* is a food stand or eatery, such as a *buffet de la gare* at a train station. A *bar à vin,* or wine bar, offers light sandwiches and salads along with wine. You could also choose a *salon de thé,* a tearoom, where delectable pastries and light snacks are available along with coffee, tea and hot chocolate. Some *pâtisseries,* or pastry shops, have a few tables and chairs, qualifying them also as *salons de thé.* Many bread and pastry shops do a lively take-out business at lunch, selling a variety of sandwiches and quiches as well as bottled drinks. And at the very-high end are *restaurants gastronomiques* whose staffs take pride in elevating gastronomy to a fine art.

The French draw a fine distinction between the words *carte* and *menu. La carte* is the English equivalent of a menu, with a comprehensive list of the establishment's offerings. *Le menu,* however, is best described as a meal plan, also sometimes referred to as *la formule* or formula. Diners order a series of dishes for a fixed price, typically an appetizer (*entrée*), a main course (*plat principal*), and a cheese course or dessert. A beverage, such as wine or coffee, may be included in the price, or cost extra. There is usually an opportunity to choose from several options within each category. The daily specials (*plats du jour*) are often listed on a chalkboard or slate (*ardoise*) in front of the restaurant or on a sheet of paper inside the standard menu. Of course, you can always order *à la carte* but it's a good idea to follow the lead of the locals. If they're ordering the *plat du jour,* chances are it's a reliable choice.

A *couvert* means a table setting—fork, knife, spoon and napkin. Service is included in the bill (*l'addition* or *la note*) and it is not necessary to leave anything more. But waiters or *serveurs* (no longer called *garçons,* but *monsieur, mademoiselle* or *madame*) will always appreciate it if you add a few extra coins when you pay for the meal.

Smoking is prohibited in all restaurants (and public buildings) across the country, but permitted at outdoor tables. If you are a non-smoker (*non-fumeur*), it is best not to sit downwind.

If you are taking your coffee on the run, you might want to stand at a café's counter. Because there is no table service involved, you'll save a few *centîmes* on the price of your *espresso* or *grand crème.* (For the differences in coffee drinks, see the *Foods & Flavors Guide,* p. 110.)

There is no easy answer to the question, "How do the French eat?" Lifestyles are changing in France and along with them, diet. Globalization and shifting demographic patterns have made it possible for new foods and dishes to become part of the culinary landscape. Breakfasts are becoming more substantial, with people eating yogurt and cereal as well as bread. (A

TOP LEFT An assortment of Provençal vegetable spreads from La Corbeille des Saveurs based in Grans, near Arles. **TOP RIGHT** A cheese plate served at L'Hostellerie d'Acquigny in Normandy, featuring a variety of regional cheeses. **MIDDLE** A feast of olives at one of Paris's many outdoor markets. **BOTTOM** *Fougasse,* a type of bread associated with Provence but available across France. These loaves were baked by La Boulange des Marchés and sold at Paris's rue de Raspail market.

TOP LEFT At a food show in Saulieu, in Burgundy, Arnold Marcillac of Camille des Lys, Aubrac, located in south central France, stands behind his mushrooms cured in olive oil. **TOP RIGHT** A selection of breads at Paris's Le Boulanger de Monge, a bakery that specializes in *pains biologiques et pains de tradition,* organic and traditional breads. **BOTTOM** Milk-fed veal chops prepared by chef François Deduit at L'Hostellerie du Moulin Fouret in Normandy.

TOP LEFT Early-season melons at the rue Mouffetard market, one of Paris's oldest and most colorful places to shop. **TOP RIGHT** *Sablé aux fraises et rhubarbe,* strawberry and rhubarb tart at L'Hostellerie d'Acquigny in Normandy. **MIDDLE** Christian Constant's *pâtisseries* are irresistible at his Left Bank Paris chocolate and pastry shop. **BOTTOM** *Porcelet rôti au jus avec radis confits et petites carrottes,* roast pork with glazed radishes and baby carrots served family-style at L'Auberge de la Ruchotte near Beaune.

TOP LEFT Elegant white asparagus and baby spinach spell spring at outdoor markets like this one in Paris. **TOP RIGHT** Rounds of *tomme de chèvre* (goat cheese) at Lyon's scenic Marché du Quai Saint-Antoine, along the Saône river. **MIDDLE** Tiny "pigeon heart" tomatoes grown in Brittany and brought to market in Rennes. **BOTTOM** Vineyards in the Languedoc-Roussillon region along the Mediterranean recall France's early wine-growing history, dating back to the 5th century BCE.

TOP LEFT *Poissonneries,* or fish markets, across France offer a wide selection of fresh fish and shellfish. Here, red mullet (*rouget barbet*), a popular fish associated with the Mediterranean, and *araignées,* or spider crabs, are beautifully displayed. **TOP RIGHT** A fishmonger slices smoked salmon to order at Paris's rue Raspail market. **BOTTOM** Presentation is always important. A simple salad course can be as colorful and refreshing as this one, accompanied by a pitcher of raspberry balsamic vinaigrette.

TOP LEFT Patrick Ramelet shows off his *sorbet au fromage blanc* at the chef's Auberge du Beau-Lieu in Normandy. **TOP RIGHT** *Cocotte d'épaule d'agneau au citron confit,* stewed lamb shoulder, at L'Hostellerie d'Acquigny in Normandy. **BOTTOM RIGHT** *Filet de loup à l'aneth et pastis,* a fillet of sea bass with dill, prepared by Bridget Pugh, Le Bistro à Vin's executive chef in Montpeyroux. **BOTTOM** *Sandre au vin rouge,* a fish similar to perch in a red-wine sauce, made by chef Patrick Auduc at La Vieille Auberge, Saulieu.

TOP LEFT A delicious chocolate and banana tart prepared by chocolatier Christian Constant at his Paris shop. **TOP RIGHT** *Brandade de morue en feuilleté,* or creamed salt cod in a puff pastry crust, made by Erick Vedel at his cooking school in Arles. **BOTTOM** Dining al fresco can be magical at places like the Domaine de Chichery, a 14th-century residence where Here on the Spot chef Peter Shaw and his wife Sally cater gourmet food holidays.

TOP LEFT This amusing restaurant along Paris's rue Monge calls attention to its homemade onion soup and Burgundy snails. **TOP RIGHT** Many restaurants in Paris, such as this one along the Boulevard du Port-Royal, specialize in regional cuisine. **MIDDLE RIGHT** Marie Bourut, of the Manoir du Val in Normandy, stands in her apple orchard holding a bottle of her Calvados. **BOTTOM** *Dos de sandre* (a fish similar to perch) with a butter and white-wine sauce and asparagus, made by chef Stéphane Derbord at his restaurant in Dijon.

small section of bread sliced in half lengthwise, served with butter, jam or a hazelnut spread, is more typical than a croissant.) While adults may drink coffee or tea for breakfast, the children are given hot chocolate. Eating habits may be different if you live in urban or rural areas. In small towns, for instance, the French may still go home for lunch between 12 and 2 PM. Restaurants may only serve within that time frame, although cafés will still be open, providing more limited menus, such as a baguette sandwich of ham and/or cheese. Outside of large urban areas, local food shops will remain open during the lunch hour, but may close for several hours thereafter before resuming operation later in the day.

A few words about wine and cheese—in fine restaurants, *sommeliers,* or wine stewards, can guide you to a wine that will fit both your menu choices and your budget. The *sommelier* can also help you choose a good local wine. At less fancy establishments, there is no shame in ordering the house wine, although the quality will vary from place to place. You can ask for a carafe or pitcher (*pichet*). *Un quart de litre* equals about one and a half glasses of wine.

Cheeses are grouped according to their provenance: cow, ewe or goat. Some cheeses are made with raw milk (*lait cru*), as many French believe that pasteurization kills bacteria essential to the taste of a cheese. Some of these cheeses can go to market after aging for less than 60 days, the time frame required by law in the US. In France, raw-milk Camembert can go to market after three weeks of aging, but today about 90% of Camembert cheeses are made from pasteurized milk. Cheeses are high in fat, but the luxurious *triple-crèmes,* such as Brillat-Savarin, top the charts at 75% butterfat. Some *tomme* cheeses, however, are made with skim milk and are particularly delectable despite their low-fat content.

The French usually drink water along with wine at both lunch and dinner. There are two kinds of bottled water to choose from—still (*plate*) and fizzy (*gazeuse*)—as well as a pitcher of ordinary tap water (*une carafe d'eau*). French tap water (*eau de robinet*) is generally safe to drink, but when traveling, it is wise not to take the chance of ruining a vacation because of differences in local water. We encourage travelers to stick to bottled or canned beverages.

As you order from the menu, some key words to look for are *maison,* house-made, which means food made on the premises, and *terroir,* which suggests the dish or the ingredients are from the land (*terre*) or the area. *Terroir* connotes high quality and traditional practices. Also see the *Foods & Flavors Guide* for translations of particular ingredients or preparation styles.

EXCELLENT   **aïgo bouïdo** Provençal garlic soup made with garlic, bacon, potato, egg and olive oil. The name means "boiled water," in the Occitan language.

aiguillettes de canard long, thin pieces of sautéed duck fillets.

aiguillettes de poulet panées au pain d'épices fried chicken cutlets with a gingerbread crust (see recipe, p. 56).

DELICIOUS   **aile de raie** skate wing, poached or sautéed, served with lemon juice, brown butter and sometimes capers.

aioli garlic mayonnaise, served as an appetizer along with raw vegetables, as a dish including boiled vegetables and meat or poultry, or as an accompaniment to fish soups such as *bourride*.

aligot potatoes whipped with cheese and garlic.

anchoïade anchovy paste, made with garlic, olives, tomatoes, olive oil and herbs, often served spread on toast, as an appetizer, or with a salad, as a light meal.

GOOD CHOICE   **anchois de Collioure sur leur nid de poivrons grillés** anchovies served on a bed of grilled peppers. The small fish is a specialty of Collioure, a fishing town on the Mediterranean.

andouille pork or chitterling sausage, often labeled "de Vire" or "de Guémené" for communities, respectively in Normandy and Brittany, where these traditional sausages have been made for several centuries. It is usually served as a first course.

andouillette pork or chitterling sausage smaller than *andouille*. A specialty of eastern France, the meat is often grilled and served with mustard and mashed or scalloped potatoes. Look for sausage rated AAAAA, or "5A," the stamp of approval of the Association Amicale des Amateurs d'Andouillettes Authentiques, an association devoted to promoting authentic *andouillette* sausage.

andouillette moutarde à l'ancienne sausage and onions with mustard sauce, done the old-fashioned way.

artichauts en ragoût de citron artichokes marinated in lemon juice.

asperges blanches au jambon white asparagus and ham. Alsace is famous for its white asparagus and there this dish may be served along with three different sauces: oil and vinegar dressing or vinaigrette, hollandaise sauce and *sauce mousseline* (hollandaise sauce lightened with whipped cream).

asperges vapeur steamed asparagus, often served cold with mayonnaise as a first course.

asperges vertes du Pertuis cuites à la minute green asparagus from Le Pertuis in Provence, given a very quick cooking.

assiette anglaise assorted cold cuts.

assiette de charcuterie plate of assorted sausages. GOOD CHOICE

assiette de crudités plate of sliced or grated vegetables, such as NATIONAL FAVORITE raw tomatoes, carrots, cucumbers and cooked beets, served with an accompanying sauce or salad dressing.

assiette de jambon de pays plate of country-style ham, sometimes from the region.

assiette du pêcheur fisherman's plate, meaning a variety of cooked fish and/or shellfish.

assiette landaise see *salade landaise.*

aubergines grillées grilled eggplant.

avocat cocktail aux crevettes avocado appetizer served on a bed of lettuce with cocktail sauce, topped with shrimp.

avocat farci aux crabes et aux crevettes avocado stuffed with crabmeat and shrimp.

baba au rhum yeast pastry infused with sugar syrup and rum. DELICIOUS

baeckeofe slow-cooked stew of pork, lamb, beef and potatoes—a REGIONAL CLASSIC classic dish from the Alsace region. Also spelled *bäkeofe;* many alternative spellings are possible.

bar rôti roasted sea bass, sometimes in a salt crust (*en croûte de sel*).

baudroie fish stew from southern France. REGIONAL CLASSIC

baudroie rôtie roast monkfish, a Mediterranean specialty, sometimes served with a *beurre de Montpellier,* a cross between an herb butter and herb mayonnaise, including mustard, lemon juice, garlic, capers and anchovies.

bavarois rich custard dessert made with whipped cream, gelatin, fruit and flavorings. It is also a savory dish with gelatin, cheese and other ingredients. Also called *crème bavaroise.*

bavette d'aloyau grillée grilled sirloin steak. GOOD CHOICE

bifteck à la minute minute steak.

bifteck haché hamburger.

biscuits de langoustine fish and crayfish flan (see recipe, p. 45).

bisque de homard cream of lobster soup.

bisque d'écrevisses cream of shrimp soup.

blanc de poireaux ravigote d'herbes steamed leeks (the white parts) usually served cold in an herb vinaigrette.

blanc-manger aux asperges fresh cheese flan with asparagus.

blanquette classic stew in a white cream sauce, with onions and mushrooms, usually made with veal but also lamb or poultry.

blettes au gratin Swiss chard baked in a béchamel sauce topped with cheese. It is also called *gratin de blettes*.

EXTRAORDINARY **bloc de foie gras** block or large slice of duck or goose liver, usually served with toast.

REGIONAL CLASSIC **bœuf bourguignon** beef stew with wine sauce, a Burgundian specialty (see recipe, p. 48).

bœuf braisé beef braised or browned in butter or oil, then stewed with vegetables.

REGIONAL CLASSIC **bœuf carbonnade** braised beef stewed in beer and onions. The dish comes from northern France.

bœuf en daube beef stew, cooked traditionally in a *daubière* or earthenware dish, and served with macaroni or potatoes.

bœuf miroton beef and onion stew.

bouchée-à-la-reine puff pastry shell (*vol-au-vent*) filled with creamed chicken and mushrooms, typically available for takeout from a shop rather than in a restaurant.

boudin aux pommes en croûte de moutarde blood sausage with apples, topped with mustard breadcrumbs.

REGIONAL CLASSIC **bouillabaisse** classic Mediterranean fish soup or chowder that traditionally includes scorpion fish (*rascasse*).

GOOD CHOICE **boules de Picolat** Catalonian meatballs, with a tomato paste and green olive sauce flavored with cinnamon.

boulettes beef or lamb croquettes.

bourride Mediterranean fish soup made with onions, garlic, tomatoes and saffron and served with aïoli.

DELICIOUS **brandade de morue** salt cod and potato purée (see recipe, p. 55). The dish can be served as a spread or as a main course baked inside a puff pastry crust.

REGIONAL CLASSIC **bréjaude** hearty cabbage and potato soup from the Limousin region in southwestern France, usually served with a piece of salt pork.

brochette de bœuf chunks of beef grilled on a skewer, sometimes with vegetables.

brouillade d'œuf à la truffe noire fancy scrambled egg dish with black truffles.

buffet de charcuterie selection of cold cuts.

buffet de fruits de mer selection of shellfish, the "fruits of the sea."

EXCELLENT **cailles aux raisins** roast quail with green grapes.

caillette d'agneau lamb sausage, a specialty of Provence and the Languedoc-Roussillon.

canard à l'orange duck with orange sauce.

canard Col Vert aux figues fraîches et poivre noir "green-collared" or mallard duck served with fresh figs and ground black pepper.

cargolade dish of grilled snails and sometimes sausages, a specialty of the Languedoc region in southern France.

carpaccio thinly sliced fish, shellfish, meat, poultry or vegetables.

carré d'agneau en croûte d'herbes rack of lamb in an herb crust (see recipe, p. 56). **DELICIOUS**

carré d'agneau forestière roast rack of lamb, served with potatoes and mushrooms.

cassolette de Coquilles Saint-Jacques scallop casserole.

cassoulet rich white-bean stew from southwestern France, made with a variety of meats, including duck, goose, pork or mutton. **REGIONAL CLASSIC**

céleri remoulade grated celery root in a mustard mayonnaise.

cervelle de Canut an appetizer or dip made of *fromage blanc*, a soft, white cheese, with the addition of shallots, oil and vinegar and seasonings. The name, which means "silk weavers' brains," is a reference to the once-lively silk-weaving industry of Lyon, where the dish is a specialty. **GREAT**

charlotte aux pommes apple charlotte.

chaud-froid de fruits rouges baked fruit dessert, served hot with ice cream, hence the reference to hot and cold. The dish usually includes red fruits such as raspberries, strawberries or currants. **GOOD CHOICE**

chaudrée North Atlantic fish chowder; a meal in itself.

chausson au Camembert et aux pommes pastry crust filled with Camembert cheese and apples.

chausson de faisan pheasant baked in a "slipper" of pastry crust.

chèvre frais aux petits légumes croquants fresh goat's-milk cheese served with small pieces of vegetables, either raw or briefly sautéed and still crunchy.

chou farci stuffed cabbage.

chou rouge stewed red cabbage.

choucroute garnie sauerkraut with potatoes, pork hock and sausage. It is originally from the Alsace region but now found in bistros across France. **DELICIOUS**

choux chantilly cream puffs filled with whipped cream.

civet game stewed in red wine, with vegetables.

civet de lièvre à la forestière rabbit stew, prepared forest-style, with mushrooms and diced potatoes fried in butter. **EXCELLENT**

civet de marcassin braised wild baby boar, under six months old.

civet de sanglier wild boar stew.

NATIONAL FAVORITE **clafoutis** deep-dish fruit flan traditionally made with cherries (often unpitted) but also other fruits, such as pears, apricots and berries. It is a specialty of the Limousin region in southwestern France. Also called *clafouti*.

cocotte de fruits au vin épicé fruits poached in mulled wine, served in a small casserole or ramekin (see recipe, p. 62).

cœurs à la crème sweet cheese dessert served with fruit.

colin crème de basilic hake with a basil cream sauce.

REGIONAL CLASSIC **confit de canard landais et pommes sautées** preserved duck, cooked in its own fat then covered in fat to keep it from coming in contact with air. This dish comes from the Landes region of southwestern France and is served with fried potatoes.

confit d'oignons preserved onions, or onion marmalade. The onions are cooked slowly with sugar, wine, vinegar and herbs. It is usually served as a side dish or accompaniment to a main dish.

GOOD CHOICE **coq au vin** capon or sometimes an old hen, stewed in wine (see recipe, p. 50).

DELICIOUS **coquilles Saint-Jacques** scallops poached, then served in their shell, often with a creamy Mornay cheese sauce.

coquilles Saint-Jacques bonne femme scallops poached or prepared simply, in the manner of the "good wife," and served with mushrooms and small onions.

côte de bœuf rib steak.

côtes d'agneau grillées aux herbes grilled lamb chops with herbs.

REGIONAL CLASSIC **cotriade** potato, fish and onion soup, topped with bread, sometimes referred to as a *Breton bouillabaisse*.

coupe de fraises a cup of strawberries, typically served with whipped cream, liqueur, ice cream or *sabayon* custard (see *Foods & Flavors Guide*).

NATIONAL FAVORITE **couscous** North African stew with vegetables, including chickpeas, and a choice of meat, chicken or sausage, served with tiny steamed pasta.

crème anglaise custard.

crème au chocolat chocolate pudding.

crème brûlée baked custard with a burnt sugar crust, sometimes with the additional words *à la vanille,* "made with vanilla."

NATIONAL FAVORITE **crème caramel** baked custard with caramel. The custard is poured onto a caramelized-sugar base, baked, cooled, then inverted when served. It is also called *crème renversée,* or "upside-down" custard.

crème d'asperges cream of asparagus soup.

crème de champignons cream of mushroom soup. The description may also specify the type of mushroom, such as *cèpe* or *bolete* (*Boletus edulis*).

crème de lentilles blondes cream of white lentil soup.

crème renversée baked custard with caramel. See *crème caramel*.

crêpes suzette thin pancakes cooked with butter and sugar and flambéed with cognac, traditionally Grand Marnier. **NATIONAL FAVORITE**

crevettes roses aillées shrimp served in a garlic sauce.

croquant aux amandes a biscotti-like almond cookie flavored with lemon and honey. In the Languedoc-Roussillon, where it is a specialty in the area around Saint-Paul-de-Fenouillet, the cookie is glazed with an egg wash.

croque-Madame toasted ham and cheese sandwich, served open-faced, with a fried egg on top. **NATIONAL FAVORITE**

croque-Monsieur toasted ham and cheese sandwich.

croustillant a crispy dish, either sweet or savory, made of layers of cookie or pastry and a filling.

crumble sweet (fruit) or savory (vegetable) dish with a crumbly top made with butter and flour, breadcrumbs or a cereal such as oatmeal or granola.

cuisse de lapin à la bière leg of rabbit stewed in beer.

cuisses de canard à l'ail duck legs in garlic sauce.

cuisses de canard confits preserved duck legs, cooked slowly in their own fat.

cuisses de grenouilles à la Provençale frogs' legs lightly floured, fried in olive oil and served with tomatoes, shallots, garlic and herbs such as thyme and bay leaf.

dacquoise elegant dessert made of meringues stacked and filled with buttercream or whipped cream.

daube de bœuf beef, usually boneless short ribs, stewed in wine. **GOOD CHOICE**

dégustation de fromages a selection of cheeses. **DELICIOUS**

délice aux griottes cherry delight, a cake topped with cherries or cherry jam. The dessert may also be made with *griottines,* small Morello cherries macerated in Kirsch liqueur.

demi-homard froid half of a boiled lobster, served cold, with an herb mayonnaise.

diplomate cold, molded dessert with alternating layers of ladyfingers and custard.

dos de cabillaud the back or meatiest cut of codfish.

duo de fromages cheese plate including a selection of two pieces of cheese.

échine de porc en cocotte pork shoulder cook and served in a small casserole.

entrecôte à la bordelaise grilled rib-eye or sirloin steak served in a red-wine sauce.

GOOD CHOICE **entrecôte grillée** grilled rib-eye or sirloin steak.

entrecôte maître d'hôtel grilled rib-eye or sirloin steak with butter and parsley.

épaule d'agneau à la boulangère roast lamb shoulder served with potatoes and onions.

escabèche de sardines marinated raw sardines.

escalope de dinde fried turkey cutlet.

EXCELLENT **escalope de foie gras poêlée au chutney de pommes vertes** fried duck or goose liver served with green apple chutney.

REGIONAL CLASSIC **escalopes de veau à la normande** veal cutlets prepared with cider and cream.

escalopes de veau aux girolles veal cutlets sautéed and served with chanterelle mushrooms.

escalopes de veau panées au parmesan veal cutlets coated in breadcrumbs and Parmesan cheese and fried.

escargots de Bourgogne snails baked in garlic butter and chopped parsley, topped with breadcrumbs, often served on a special plate with tongs and a two-pronged fork. Despite the name, the snails are unlikely to be the Burgundy variety but instead the *petit* or *gros gris,* harvested or farm-raised in Burgundy or elsewhere.

VERY POPULAR **faisselle de chèvre frais aux herbes fines** fresh goat's-milk cheese with fresh herbs.

farandole gourmande choice of several desserts.

faux-filet avec pommes frites grilled steak with French fries, a popular bistro or brasserie dish.

faux-filet sauce poivre ou Roquefort steak with pepper or Roquefort cheese sauce.

figue farcie au foie gras figs stuffed with duck or goose liver, served with salad.

filet de bœuf grillé béarnaise sirloin steak, grilled, served with a béarnaise sauce.

filet de canard aux clémentines breast of duck with clementines.

filet de daurade royale oven-baked fillet of sea bream, a fish similar to porgy.

filet de loup à l'aneth et pastis sea bass fillet with dill and pastis, an anise-flavored aperitif (see recipe, p. 49). **DELICIOUS**

filet de rosbif en croûte de sel roast beef baked in a salt crust.

filet de rouget en papillote red mullet baked or steamed in parchment paper.

filet de sandre meunière fillet of freshwater fish, similar to perch or pike, cooked in the style of the miller's wife (*meunière*)— lightly floured and fried in butter. Served with chopped parsley and lemon slices.

filet mignon de sanglier aux marrons boar steak, either grilled or sautéed, served with chestnuts.

filets de hareng pommes de terre tièdes herring pickled in brine, served with warm boiled potatoes. **GOOD CHOICE**

flamiche similar to a quiche, but made with a pizza-like bread dough, filled with eggs, cream, cheese and leeks. The dish comes from northern and eastern France. **REGIONAL CLASSIC**

flammeküeche bacon and onion pie from eastern France.

foie de veau calf's liver, lightly sautéed, usually served with a garnish of parsley.

foie de volailles chicken liver.

foie gras de canard duck liver, usually served with chutney or fruit to complement the richness of the dish. It is often *mi-cuit,* or lightly cooked, and may come with toast. **EXCELLENT**

foie gras d'oie goose liver.

foie gras poêlé pan-fried duck or goose liver.

fondant au chocolat coulant pistache gooey chocolate cake filled with a pistachio and white-chocolate sauce that oozes out of the cake when it is eaten. **HEAVENLY**

fondant aux framboises gooey raspberry cake.

fondant de foies de volailles creamy chicken-liver spread.

fonds d'artichauts artichoke hearts, which may be served with a vinaigrette or other sauce.

fraises au sucre fresh strawberries with sugar.

fricassée de pintade guinea hen braised in white sauce or butter. **EXCELLENT**

fricassou de légumes à l'huile d'olive vegetables sautéed in olive oil.

frites maison homemade French fries.

friture de limande pan-fried lemon sole.

fromage frais "fresh cheese," a soft, white cheese (also called *fromage blanc*) made from cow's milk, and similar to a creamed cottage cheese. It is often served as a dessert with honey, (*au miel*), with maple syrup (*au sirop d'érable*) or with fruit.

galette de brandade de morue codfish cake.

galette de pommes de terre potato pancake.

REGIONAL CLASSIC   **galettes bretonnes au sarrasin** thin Brittany buckwheat pancakes, with ham, cheese and egg (either scrambled or sunny-side up).

gambas flambées au whisky large shrimp or prawns sautéed and flamed with whiskey, possibly with garlic, parsley and cream added. Other liqueurs may be substituted.

REGIONAL CLASSIC   **garbure** cabbage soup or stew served with a piece of bread spread with a savory filling.

gaspacho de fraises cold strawberry soup, served as dessert.

gâteau au chocolat chocolate cake.

EXTRAORDINARY   **gâteau basque** two-crust tart with custard in the middle, from the Basque region in southwestern France.

DELICIOUS   **gâteau breton** simple but rich butter cake from the Brittany region in western France.

gâteau de riz rice pudding.

NATIONAL FAVORITE   **gigot d'agneau** roast leg of lamb, often served with *flageolets,* small white beans.

glace chantilly ice cream with whipped cream.

glaces au choix choice of ice cream.

glaces et sorbets ice creams and sherbets. Menus will often indicate whether these are made on the premises or come from a renowned purveyor, such as Berthillon.

GOOD CHOICE   **gougère** cheese puff, served as an appetizer, originally from Burgundy but ubiquitous.

gras-double de bœuf à la bourgeoise tripe (beef stomach) stewed with carrots and onions.

gras-double de bœuf frit pané tripe (beef stomach) cut into pieces, breaded and fried.

REGIONAL CLASSIC   **gratin dauphinois** scalloped potatoes, from the Dauphiné region in east central France (see recipe, p. 59).

gratin de blettes Swiss chard baked in a béchamel sauce and topped with cheese. It is also called *blettes au gratin*.

gratin de framboises a popular dessert of raspberries topped with
custard and oven-broiled to give the dish a lightly browned and
crispy crust.

gratin d'endives baked endive in a béchamel sauce.

gratinée French onion soup that originated in Lyon, although
Paris would probably want to claim credit.

hachis parmentier cottage pie, a hash of ground beef with a
mashed potato topping.

harengs marinés aux pommes vapeur herring marinated in
vinegar, onions, carrots and herbs, served with steamed potatoes.

haricots verts frais garden-fresh French green beans, usually
steamed and served with butter.

homard à l'armoricaine also referred to as *homard à l'américaine*.
The dish is associated with l'Armorique, a region of Brittany,
but it may be a Provençal creation rather than a Breton or
American one. Whatever the name, the method of preparation
for the dish appears to be the same—raw lobster sautéed in
olive oil, with onions, shallots, tomatoes and garlic.

homard thermidor classic dish of lobster split in half lengthwise,
grilled or roasted, and served in its shell with a cream sauce.
There is no consensus on who created the dish or when,
whether it was prepared for Napoleon during the month of
Thermidor (mid-July to mid-August according to the French
Republican calendar) or in conjunction with the Paris premiere
of a play by the same name.

huîtres oysters, usually served raw. The menu will indicate how
many to an order. (Be advised that eating raw or under-cooked
foods may increase the risk of food-borne illness.) See p. 27 for
more about types of oysters.

huîtres en nage oysters swimming in cream.

huîtres gratinées baked dish of oysters, garlic, breadcrumbs and
grated cheese.

île flottante dessert featuring one large meringue swimming in
crème anglaise or English custard, with caramelized sugar on
top; similar to *œufs à la neige*.

jambon cru smoked, uncooked ham.

jambon de Paris boiled ham. Also called *jambon blanc*.

jambon de pays country-style ham. Also called *jambon de campagne*.

jambon sec cured ham.

jambonneau en salade de lentilles tièdes pork knuckle and warm lentil salad.

jambonnettes de cuisses de grenouille stuffed frog's legs.

GOOD CHOICE **jarret d'agneau** braised lamb shank.

jarret de porc au raifort pork hock with horseradish.

jarret de veau veal shank.

joues de sanglier stewed wild boar cheeks.

REGIONAL CLASSIC **kig ha farz** hot pot of pork, beef and vegetables, with buckwheat dumplings. The dish is a specialty of the Brittany region in western France.

REGIONAL CLASSIC **kouign-aman** traditional Brittany cake made from a yeast dough, layered with butter, formed into a round loaf and glazed with egg and sugar. It is also spelled *kouign-amann*.

DELICIOUS **lapin à l'oseille** rabbit cooked with sorrel and thickened with crème fraîche. (For a recipe, see p. 51.)

lapin au cidre rabbit stewed in hard cider.

lapin fauve au miel et vinaigre de vin wild rabbit or hare stewed with honey and wine vinegar.

lasagnes de saumon aux épinards en terrine salmon and spinach lasagna served in an earthenware dish.

NATIONAL FAVORITE **lentilles tièdes** lentil salad. Sometimes called France's potato salad, it is served warm as a first course or as a side dish with roast pork or ham.

lièvre à la royale wild hare in a blood and gizzard sauce.

EXCELLENT **lotte rôtie** roasted monkfish.

macédoine de fruits mixed fruit or fruit salad.

macédoine de légumes mixed vegetables.

DELICIOUS **magret de canard** duck breast, cooked pink and served in thin slices or *aiguillettes,* often with a fruit or honey sauce.

mara des bois avec double crème type of strawberry served with heavy cream.

marmite dieppoise shellfish and fish stew from Dieppe, along the Normandy coast. The fish is often turbot and sole, but can also include salmon. — REGIONAL CLASSIC

médaillons de biche à la crème medallions of venison in cream sauce.

merguez spicy lamb sausages, brought to France by North African immigrants. *Merguez* is popular across the country and often served with couscous, but also with French fries. — GOOD CHOICE

mignons de veau fermier small veal cutlets floured and fried in butter.

millefeuille classic dessert, much like a Napoleon, named "thousand leaves" to describe the layers of puff pastry, which are filled with pastry cream. It may be served with fresh fruit (*aux fruit frais*) and a *crème anglaise* flavored with liqueur, such as Grand Marnier. A *millefeuille* may also be a savory dish featuring a number of layers and a variety of ingredients. — DELICIOUS

miroton stew made with cooked meat and onions. *Miroton,* also spelled *mironton,* can also refer to a fruit compote.

mitonnée de joue de porc stewed pork cheeks.

moelleux à la banane gooey banana cake.

moelleux au chocolat gooey chocolate cake. — DELICIOUS

morue Île-de-France salt cod cooked in white wine.

mouclade steamed mussels with shallots and garlic sautéed in butter, saffron and curry. It is a specialty of the Poitou-Charentes region in western France. — GOOD CHOICE

moules à la crème steamed mussels with cream.

moules au cidre mussels steamed in hard cider.

moules marinières mussels steamed in white wine, a dish found across the country but associated with mussel-growing grounds, such as along the Atlantic coast. — NATIONAL FAVORITE

mousse au chocolat chocolate mousse. — NATIONAL FAVORITE

mystère ice cream dessert with meringue and cake.

navarin d'agneau lamb stew, often served with spring vegetables (*à la printanière*). — EXCELLENT

nouzillards au lait chestnuts cooked in milk. The dish, associated with the Anjou region in central France, was once a simple dinner meal eaten by country people. — GOOD CHOICE

œuf à la coque soft-boiled egg, served in the shell.

œuf brouillé scrambled egg.

œuf cocotte au crabe coddled egg with crab, or an egg dish baked in the oven in a small dish or ramekin.

œuf cocotte au saumon fumé coddled or baked egg along with smoked salmon.

œuf cocotte aux crevettes coddled or baked egg with shrimp.

œuf dûr mayonnaise hard-boiled egg and mayonnaise, typically served on a bed of lettuce; a popular appetizer in bistros and brasseries.

GOOD CHOICE **œuf en gelée** poached egg in aspic, with ham and chives.

REGIONAL CLASSIC **œuf en meurette** poached egg with red-wine and mushroom sauce. This is a classic Burgundian dish, usually served as a first course.

œuf mollet soft-boiled egg, served out of the shell.

œuf poché poached egg.

DELICIOUS **œufs à la neige** "eggs in snow." Sweetened egg whites poached in milk, served with vanilla custard. It is similar to *île flottante*.

œufs de truites rouges trout roe.

EXCELLENT **omelette au fromage** cheese omelet.

omelette au jambon ham omelet.

omelette aux champignons mushroom omelet.

omelette aux fines herbes omelet with herbs, including chives, chervil and parsley. It is a staple of French cuisine.

EXCELLENT **omelette fourrée aux pommes** sweet omelet filled with cooked apples. Also called *omelette normande*.

omelette landaise omelet with pine nuts.

omelette nature plain omelet.

omelette normande sweet omelet filled with cooked apples. Also called *omelette fourrée aux pommes*.

omelette norvégienne baked Alaska.

omelette paysanne "peasant-style" omelet with potatoes and bacon.

GOOD CHOICE **onglet aux échalotes** skirt steak with shallots.

orange pressée fresh-squeezed orange juice.

os à la moelle beef bone marrow.

paillard de dinde turkey cutlet.

paillard de veau veal cutlet.

pain perdu French toast.

paleron de bœuf lardé braised shoulder of beef, threaded with lard and served with mushrooms.

palette de porc rôtie roasted pork shoulder.

palombe rôtie aux cèpes et foie gras roast wood pigeon, served with mushrooms and duck, goose or chicken liver.

panaché de barbue et de lieu jaune fish medley, including *barbue,* which is similar to flounder, and *lieu,* which is similar to pollock or cod. GOOD CHOICE

pan-bagnat popular round white-bread sandwich filled with olives, tomatoes, anchovies and hard-boiled egg. The sandwich is a specialty of the area around Nice. The name translates literally to moist bread. Also spelled *pan bagna.* REGIONAL CLASSIC

pannequet de saumon fumé smoked salmon "wrap" with trout eggs (see recipe, p. 52).

parfait de foies de volaille chicken-liver purée.

Paris-Brest wheel- or crown-shaped cream puff, traditionally filled with praline buttercream, but also whipped cream. It takes its name from a bicycle race between Brest, in Brittany, and Paris, first run in 1891. NATIONAL FAVORITE

parmentier de canard shredded duck, sometimes embellished with duck or goose liver, with a crusty mashed potato and cheese topping.

pâté de campagne rustic or country-style meat loaf. The dish is also called *terrine de campagne.*

pâté de truffes truffle spread (see recipe, p. 46).

pâté en croûte meat loaf, made with pork and/or veal, baked in a pastry crust.

pâté maison home-style meat loaf. DELICIOUS

pâtisserie au choix choice of pastry.

pâtisserie du jour pastry or dessert of the day.

pâtisserie maison pastry dessert made in-house.

paupiettes de veau thin slices of veal stuffed with a meat and vegetable filling. GOOD CHOICE

pavé de biche aux cèpes venison steak with bolete mushrooms.

pavé de turbot roasted turbot steak, in the shape of a brick or paving stone. Cod (*cabillaud*) and bass (*loup de mer*) are also served this way. GOOD CHOICE

pêches Melba classic dessert of poached peaches, raspberry sauce and vanilla ice cream created in the 1890s by French chef Auguste Escoffier in honor of opera singer Nellie Melba.

petit salé aux lentilles salt-cured belly of pork served with lentils.

petits farcis stuffed vegetables, such as red pepper, tomato or zucchini. This is another delectable Provençal dish.

pièce de bœuf au poivre mignonnette et flambée beef steak with coarsely ground white pepper, flamed with liqueur.

pied de porc pork trotters.

pilaf rice dish.

EXCELLENT **pipérade** vegetable and egg dish made with onions, tomatoes and red peppers. The eggs may be scrambled in a stew of the vegetables, or the vegetables may be served in an omelet. *Pipérade* is derived from the Basque word *piper,* meaning "red pepper."

piquenchâgne double-crust pear pie or pear bread, a specialty of the Auvergne region in central France. In neighboring districts it is also called *poirat*.

REGIONAL CLASSIC **pissaladière** French-style pizza native to southeastern France, made with anchovies, garlic, onions and olives. *Pissaladière* is derived from the word *pissalat,* meaning "salted fish."

DELICIOUS **Pithiviers** puff-pastry tart filled with almond paste, originally from Pithiviers, in the Loire Valley. It is also a lark pâté.

plateau de charcuterie platter of cold cuts.

plateau de fruits de mer platter of seafood ("fruits of the sea") such as oysters, clams and other shellfish.

poêlée de cèpes à l'échalotte pan-seared mushrooms with shallots.

poêlée de cuisses de dindonneau pan-seared or sautéed turkey thighs.

poêlée de thon pan-seared or sautéed tuna.

poêlée de veau au persil pan-seared veal roast with parsley.

poirat double-crust pear pie. It is also called *piquenchâgne*.

GOOD CHOICE **poireaux à la vinaigrette** braised leeks, served cold in a vinaigrette—a bistro classic.

GOOD CHOICE **poires pochées** poached pears, often with spices (*aux épices*) or in red wine (*au vin rouge*).

poitrine de porc pork belly.

poitrine de veau farcie stuffed breast of veal.

pommes allumettes matchstick-size fried potatoes.

pommes boulangère gratin of potatoes and onions, served with roast beef or lamb.

ELEGANT **pommes de terre Anna** dish similar to scalloped potatoes.

pommes de terre en robe des champs baked potato.

pommes de terre primeurs au vinaigre fingerling potatoes tossed in white wine and vinegar.

pommes écrasées mashed potatoes, which are also called *purée de pommes de terre* and *pressée de pommes de terre*.

pommes frites French fries.

pommes pailles straw-thin or shoestring fried potatoes.

pommes rissolées pan-fried potatoes.

pommes vapeur steamed potatoes.

porc aux pruneaux pork roast stuffed with prunes, a specialty of   DELICIOUS
the Touraine in the Loire region.

porcelet rôti au jus avec radis confits et petites carottes roast
suckling pig served with glazed radishes and baby carrots (see
recipe, p. 53).

potage country-style soup.

potage Crécy carrot soup, usually including onions, leeks and
potatoes. Two eponymous towns in France, one in Picardie, the
other in the Île-de-France, claim credit for the soup, but it is
found across the country. The soup may also appear on menus
as *purée de Crécy*.

potage cressonnière watercress soup.

potage parmentier classic leek and potato soup, served hot.   NATIONAL FAVORITE

potage printanier vegetable soup.

potage Saint-Germain split pea soup.

pot-au-feu hearty stew of boiled meat and vegetables, such as   NATIONAL FAVORITE
carrots, turnips, cabbage, leeks and potatoes. Traditionally, the
cuts of meat were not expensive and therefore needed to be
cooked slowly over the stove to become tender and release their
juices. Hence the name, which means "pot on the fire." *Pot-au-
feu* is classic French comfort food. The broth is served as a soup,
separate from the meats and vegetables.

pot-de-crème baked custard dessert in various flavors, such as
vanilla, coffee or chocolate, served in individual ramekins.

potée hearty stew, usually including cabbage and potatoes but   GOOD CHOICE
sometimes pork, traditionally cooked in an earthenware pot.

poule au pot hen poached with carrots, celery and potatoes. *Poule*   GOOD CHOICE
au pot was once touted as a national dish. In the 16th century,
King Henry IV, worried about the health of his subjects,
declared that there would be a stewed chicken on every French
household's table once a week.

poule au riesling chicken stewed in Riesling wine, often served
with egg noodles. The dish is from the Alsace region in
northeastern France.

poule au vinaigre à l'ancienne chicken stewed in red wine vinegar.

poulet chasseur stewed chicken with mushrooms, shallots and
tomatoes. It is called *chasseur* (hunter-style) because the dish
originally was made with game.

EXCELLENT **poulet de Bresse en demi-deuil** prized variety of chicken, cooked with slices of black truffle under the skin.

poulet pommes frites piece of roast chicken with French fries.

poulet rôti roast chicken.

poulet sauté à l'estragon sautéed chicken with tarragon.

REGIONAL CLASSIC **poulet (flambé) vallée d'Auge** chicken stewed with apples and cider (or sometimes chicken stock, instead) and thickened with cream. The dish comes from the Auge valley in Normandy. Calvados (apple brandy) is sometimes used to flambé the dish.

pounti terrine or meat loaf of pork, Swiss chard and prunes.

pressée de pommes de terre mashed potatoes. They are also called *purée de pommes de terre* and *pommes écrasées*.

NATIONAL FAVORITE **profiteroles au chocolat chaud** cream puffs, usually filled with whipped or ice cream, topped with hot chocolate sauce—a bistro classic.

pruneaux au vin avec glace vanillée prunes stewed in wine, served with vanilla ice cream.

purée de carottes carrot purée.

purée de céleri celery purée.

purée de Crécy carrot soup. See *potage Crécy*.

purée de pommes de terre mashed potatoes. They are also called *pommes écrasées* and *pressée de pommes de terre*.

quatre-quarts pound cake, made with equal parts of butter, flour, sugar and eggs.

EXTRAORDINARY **quenelles de brochet** pike dumplings or balls of poached fish, often served with a crayfish sauce. The dish is a specialty of Lyon and one of the hallmarks of classic French cuisine.

DELICIOUS **quiche lorraine** classic custard pie from eastern France, made with ham or bacon, eggs and cream, but usually not cheese.

GOOD CHOICE **raclette** dish made with the eponymous cheese (see *Foods & Flavors Guide*). A block of *raclette* is heated, and the melted cheese is scraped off with a knife and served with boiled potatoes and pickles.

radis au beurre radishes served raw with bread and butter. The radishes served are usually longer and milder than the round variety. This is a popular appetizer across France, in both restaurants and homes.

ragoût de lapin à la moutarde stewed rabbit in mustard sauce.

ragoût de lapin provençal rabbit stew cooked with tomatoes, fennel and tarragon.

raie au beurre ray or skate poached in broth and served with browned butter. The fish may also be floured and fried. **EXCELLENT**

ratatouille vegetable stew made with zucchini, eggplant, tomatoes, onions, peppers, garlic and herbs. It is a specialty of southern France but found across the country. **GOOD CHOICE**

rillettes de canard duck-meat spread, cooked in fat, usually served as an appetizer.

rillettes de porc spread made of pork, fat and spices, served as an appetizer. The spread is a specialty of the region around Tours and is sometimes referred to as *rillettes de Tours*. **REGIONAL CLASSIC**

rillettes de saumon salmon spread.

rillettes d'oie goose-meat spread, cooked in fat, usually served as an appetizer.

ris de veau veal sweetbreads.

rissolé de ris de veau fried veal sweetbreads.

riz au lait à l'ancienne old-fashioned rice pudding, made with milk, sugar and sometimes egg and vanilla. **DELICIOUS**

rognonnade de veau roasted cut of veal with the kidney still attached.

rognons de veau veal kidneys, often served in a mustard sauce.

rosette de Lyon large, dried pork sausage, a specialty of Lyon.

rôti de veau veal pot roast.

rouelles de jarret de marcassin slices of leg of wild boar.

rousquille small, crown-shaped cake or cookie flavored with vanilla and glazed with sugar. It is a Spanish dessert found in southern France.

Saint-Honoré classic pastry named after the patron saint of bakers. It consists of a circle of cream puffs set on a baked puff-pastry base. The circle is then filled with pastry cream and decorated with whipped cream. **EXTRAORDINARY**

Saint-Jacques scallop dish. See *coquilles Saint-Jacques*.

salade au magret de canard fumé salad with smoked duck breast.

salade auvergnate salad with food products typical of the cooking of the Auvergne, such as sausage, bacon and cheeses such as Cantal or Fourme d'Ambert.

salade aux noix salad with walnuts.

salade composée salad composed of diverse elements, such as ham, poultry, boiled potatoes, tomatoes, much like a chef salad.

salade de betteraves cooked beets, served cold in a vinaigrette as an appetizer.

salade de cervelas salad with *cervelas* sausage and potatoes.

salade de chèvre salad with goat cheese. The cheese is often served warm with toast.

salade de cœurs de palmier aux crevettes salad with hearts of palm and boiled shrimp.

salade de crudités salad with raw vegetables such as carrots.

salade de fruits fruit salad.

salade de gésiers salad with chicken gizzards, a bistro classic.

salade de harengs herring salad.

salade de saumon fumé salad with slices of smoked salmon.

salade de tête de veau tiède salad with headcheese, a cold cut made from the head of a calf, served lukewarm.

salade de tomates tomato salad.

salade frisée aux lardons chicory or curly endive with bacon and sometimes poached egg, served with a hot vinaigrette that wilts the lettuce.

REGIONAL CLASSIC **salade landaise** green salad served with poultry gizzards, traditionally cooked in fat, and other poultry products, including liver. This salad is a specialty of the Landes region in southwestern France, which is famous for duck. Also called *assiette landaise*.

salade lyonnaise curly endive with bacon, poached egg, spring onions and croutons. It is named for its origins in Lyon.

salade mixte mixed salad.

REGIONAL CLASSIC **salade niçoise** main course salad originally from Nice that includes lettuce, tomatoes, olives, garlic, anchovies or tuna, potatoes, green beans, boiled egg and capers.

salade norvégienne salad with smoked salmon.

salade tiède aux œufs et lardons warm salad of curly endive with bacon and poached eggs, found on many bistro menus.

salade verte simple green salad, typically made with Boston-style lettuce. The salad may be served with vinaigrette or (sometimes bottled) salad dressing.

sauce for specific sauces, see *Foods & Flavors Guide*.

saucisson chaud pommes à l'huile poached sausage with boiled potatoes dressed in olive oil.

saumon à la gasconne salmon with leeks, potatoes and bacon. The dish is from the Gascony region in southwestern France.

saumon en papillotte salmon baked in parchment paper, served with an herb and wine cream sauce. GOOD CHOICE

saumon farci stuffed salmon steaks.

saumon fumé avec toasts smoked salmon with toast, a popular appetizer.

saumon mariné et tomates confites raw salmon marinated in olive oil, lemon juice and herbs, such as basil, served with slow-roasted tomatoes.

seiche aux poireaux cuttlefish (similar to squid) and leek sauté, a traditional dish of the Languedoc-Roussillon (see recipe, p. 54).

selle d'agneau à l'huile d'olive aux pommes de terre roast saddle of lamb with potatoes. GOOD CHOICE

sole bonne femme sole cooked with white wine and mushrooms.

sole meunière sole dredged in flour and fried in butter, served with lemon and parsley. This is a simple but popular dish. DELICIOUS

sole normande poached sole served with cream, a specialty of Normandy. REGIONAL CLASSIC

sorbet au fromage blanc sorbet made from *fromage blanc,* a cheese similar to ricotta.

soufflé Grand Marnier ethereal baked egg dessert made with orange-flavored brandy—one of France's great dishes. EXTRAORDINARY

soupe à la bière beer soup.

soupe à l'ail nouveau springtime garlic soup (see recipe, p. 44).

soupe à l'oignon onion soup, served with croutons and a melted cheese crust. GOOD CHOICE

soupe au pistou vegetable soup served with *pistou,* a sauce similar to pesto, made with fresh basil, garlic and olive oil. EXCELLENT

soupe aux choux cabbage soup.

soupe de poisson fish soup or stew. GOOD CHOICE

soupe jardinière garden vegetable soup.

steak au poivre pepper steak.

steak frites seared steak and French fries. Cuts of meat may vary but are typically sirloin, porterhouse or rib eye. NATIONAL FAVORITE

steak haché ground-beef patty.

steak tartare raw steak, ground or chopped fine, and served with raw egg and onions. Its name comes from Tatar or Tartar, referring to Turkic peoples of eastern Europe and Central Asia.

suprême de poulet fermier aux morilles farm-raised chicken breasts served with morel mushrooms. EXCELLENT

suprême de volaille en croûte chicken breasts baked in an herb or pastry crust.

GOOD CHOICE   **tagine** North African stew, usually made with meat but also poultry or fish. Also spelled *tajine*.

tapenade Provençal spread made of olives, capers and anchovies.

tartare de bulots au saumon fumé sliced sea snails under a bed of thinly sliced smoked salmon.

tartare de thon raw tuna cut into small pieces, served with herbs, spices, olive oil or raw egg.

tarte à la rhubarbe rhubarb tart.

REGIONAL CLASSIC   **tarte à l'oignon** Alsatian onion tart.

tarte au chocolat chocolate tart (see recipe, p. 60).

NATIONAL FAVORITE   **tarte au citron** lemon tart; an extremely popular dessert found in pastry shops and restaurants across France.

tarte au potiron pumpkin pie.

tarte au sucre sweet flat pastry, a specialty in the village of Pérouges in eastern France.

DELICIOUS   **tarte aux pommes** apple tart.

REGIONAL CLASSIC   **tarte aux pralines** tart filled with cream and pink, sugar-coated almond candies, a specialty of the region around Lyon.

tarte aux quetsches plum tart.

tarte aux tomates tomato tart.

tarte Bourdaloue pear tart. Also see *tarte fine aux poires*.

tarte fine aux poires tart made with thinly sliced pears. Also called *tarte Bourdaloue*.

tarte normande apple tart served with cream.

tarte provençale savory tart of tomatoes, olives, anchovies, garlic and herbs, from southern France. (See p. 46 for a recipe for *tarte de tomates et poivrons rouges*.)

NATIONAL FAVORITE   **tarte Tatin** upside-down apple pie said to have been invented by les demoiselles Tatin at their hotel-restaurant in Lamotte-Beuvron, south of Orléans. You can still find it served there as well as across France. When it's fresh it's delicious; when it has been sitting on the shelf for hours, it's a stodgy disappointment. (See p. 63 for a recipe for *tarte Tatin aux abricots*.)

REGIONAL CLASSIC   **tartiflette** potatoes, onions and bacon in layers, baked with cheese on top—a specialty of the French Alps.

tartine de foie gras sur mesclun toast spread or served with duck liver, accompanied by mesclun.

terrine de campagne country-style meat pâté prepared traditionally in an earthenware dish. Also called *pâté de campagne*.

terrine de canard duck pâté.

terrine de foie de volailles chicken liver paste or spread.

terrine de lapin rabbit pâté.

terrine de légumes vegetable pâté.

terrine de poisson pâté of fish, such as salmon.

terrine de veau veal pâté.

terrine du jour pâté of the day.

terrinée rice pudding. See *teurgoule.*

tête de veau sauce gribiche head of veal, served with a vinaigrette, hard-boiled eggs, capers, herbs and small pickles. It may also be served with *sauce ravigote,* a thick vinaigrette.

teurgoule rice pudding, a traditional dessert from Normandy (see recipe, p. 66). It is also referred to as *terrinée.*   REGIONAL CLASSIC

thon mayonnaise tuna steak or canned tuna with mayonnaise, a popular bistro entrée.

tian de courgettes et de tomates zucchini and tomatoes slow-cooked in a tian or earthenware casserole (see recipe, p. 60). The dish is a specialty of Provence but is found elsewhere, sometimes featuring other vegetables, such as eggplant.

tomates farcies stuffed, baked tomatoes.

tomates mozzarella slices of tomato and mozzarella.

tournedos de porc pork steaks.

tournedos Rossini center cut of beef fillet, grilled or sautéed,   EXCELLENT served with duck or goose liver and truffles.

tourte au potiron pumpkin pie.

tourte de carottes en robe de chou baked carrot and cabbage dish (see recipe, p. 58).

tourtière landaise pommes-pruneaux apple-prune tart that is a   REGIONAL CLASSIC specialty of the Landes region of Gascony in southwestern France.

travers de porcelet honey-glazed ribs from a suckling pig.

tripes à la mode de Caen classic stew from Normandy typically   REGIONAL CLASSIC made from cow's stomach, including the honeycombed reticulum, carrots, leeks, onions and cider. Not for the faint-hearted, but wonderful when prepared well.

truite au bleu trout poached in vegetable broth and wine, from   GOOD CHOICE Alsace in eastern France.

truite fraîche du vivier aux amandes freshly caught trout served with almonds.

truite meunière trout dredged in flour and fried in butter, served   GOOD CHOICE with lemon and parsley. It is a simple but popular dish.

truite pochée poached trout.

ttoro Basque fish stew made with fish fillets, shellfish, onions,   REGIONAL CLASSIC garlic, tomatoes and red and green peppers.

EXCELLENT   **vacherin** meringue dessert filled with ice cream, sweetened whipped cream and fruit. It is also a soft cow's-milk cheese from the Savoie.

velouté d'avocat cream of avocado soup with crème fraîche and shrimp.

DELICIOUS   **velouté de champignons** cream of mushroom soup.

GOOD CHOICE   **velouté de châtaignes** cream of chestnut soup.

velouté de topinambours purée of Jerusalem artichokes, or a cream soup of Jerusalem artichokes.

verrine d'avocat avocado purée or cream served in a small glass or *verrine* (see recipe, p. 48).

EXTRAORDINARY   **vichyssoise** classic cream of potato and leek soup, made famous by Ritz-Carlton chef Louis Diat, who came from the Vichy region (see recipe, p. 43).

REGIONAL CLASSIC   **waterzooi** chicken or fish stew, a specialty of northern France.

REGIONAL CLASSIC   **zewelwai** Alsatian onion and cream tart.

Foods & Flavors Guide

This chapter is a comprehensive list of foods, spices, kitchen utensils and cooking terminology in French, with English translations. Singular masculine gender *é* endings are given for adjectives without an additional *e* or *s* for feminine and plural. Both masculine and feminine forms are given only when the word substantially changes, such as *doux* (masculine) and *douce* (feminine). The list will be helpful in interpreting menus and for shopping in France's colorful and lively markets (*marchés*). As a rule, market vendors identify their products by name and by price (in euros), which is determined by weight or by the piece. In the event that the items are not identified, it is useful to learn how to say, "What is this called?" See *Helpful Phrases,* p. 75.

France is a nation of several hundred cheeses, and the names of all of them are beyond the scope of this chapter and book. So, too, are the many different kinds of wine produced in key regions around the country. For more information on cheese and wine regions, see *Regional French Foods*, p. 19. We have omitted most French words that are close to or the same as those in English. But we have included some non-French words that have become part of the country's vocabulary.

Abondance cow's-milk cheese produced in the Haute-Savoie in the Alps.

addition bill or check. Also called *la note.*

affiné ripe or aged, as in cheese. *Affinage* is the process of ripening cheese.

agneau lamb.

agrume citrus fruit.

aiglefin haddock. Also spelled *églefin.*

aigre sour.

aigre-doux (aigre-douce) sweet and sour, bittersweet.

aiguillette thin slice of poultry cut lengthwise along the breast. The term can also refer to meat.

ail garlic. *Aillade* is garlic sauce or vinaigrette, and bread rubbed with garlic and sprinkled with olive oil is called *pain à l'aillade.*

aïoli garlic mayonnaise.

airelle blueberry. Also called *myrtille*.

algue seaweed.

alimentation diet. It can also mean food or grocery stores.

allumettes matchsticks of potatoes or puff pastry.

alose shad, a saltwater fish in the herring and sardine family that spawns in rivers along France's Atlantic and Mediterranean coasts.

aloyau beef sirloin.

(à l') alsacienne prepared in the style of the Alsace region of northeastern France, typically including sauerkraut, ham and sausages.

amande almond.

amer bitter.

(à l') américaine see *(à l') armoricaine*.

amuse-bouche appetizer. Also called *amuse-gueule* (slang).

ananas pineapple.

anchois anchovy, fished in both the Atlantic and Mediterranean.

(à l') ancienne prepared in the traditional or old style, meaning cooked in a white sauce with mushrooms and onions.

andouille traditional pork or chitterling sausage, often labeled for the community where it is made.

andouillette pork or chitterling sausage smaller than *andouille*. Look for sausage rated AAAAA, or "5A," the stamp of approval of the Association Amicale des Amateurs d'Andouillettes Authentiques, an association devoted to promoting authentic *andouillette* sausage.

aneth dill.

anglaise custard made of egg yolks, milk and sugar. *À l'anglaise* refers to English cooking, meaning simple, without elaboration or particular flavor.

anguille eel.

anis aniseed. *Anis étoilé* is star anise. It is also called *badiane*.

apéritif cocktail. Also, informally, *apéro*.

appellation d'origine controlée (A.O.C.) label of origin. A.O.C. certifies that products such as cheese and wine have met strict production standards.

arachide peanut.

araignée de mer spider crab.

arête (de poisson) fish bone.

Armagnac brandy from the Armagnac region of southwestern France.

(à l') armoricaine prepared with a sauce including onion, garlic, tomato, white wine and liqueur. Sometimes used interchangeably with *américaine*.

aromates herbs, seasoning.

arrivage subject to availability.

arrosé drizzled with a liquid such as a liqueur or sauce.

asperge asparagus, most often white but also green. A purple-headed variety from Pertuis in Provence is prized.

assaisonné seasoned or seasoned with.

assiette plate. *Assiette creuse* is a soup plate.

au four oven-baked or roasted.

au jus served in its own juice or gravy.

aubergine eggplant.

avoine oats. Oatmeal is called *farine d'avoine*.

badiane star anise. Also called *anis étoilé*.

baguette the traditional French loaf of bread, thin and about 2 feet long, with a crusty outside and soft crumb inside.

baie berry.

bain marie water bath for gently warming or cooking foods.

ballotine boned, stuffed poultry.

Banon goat cheese from Provence, dipped in fruit-flavored brandy and wrapped in a chestnut leaf.

bar fish similar to bass. Also called *loup* or *loup de mer*.

barbue brill, a saltwater flatfish similar to turbot but smaller.

barquette sweet or savory tartlet in the shape of a small boat.

(à la) basquaise prepared in the style of the Basque region, characterized by tomatoes, peppers, garlic and ham.

bâtard loaf of bread, shorter and stubbier than a *baguette*.

batavia a variety of broad-leaf lettuce.

bâton stick. Refers to pastries or vegetables cut-up as sticks. It can also mean a loaf of bread smaller than a *baguette*.

bâtonnet cut-up vegetable stick larger than *allumette* or *julienne*, but smaller than *bâton*. It can also mean fish stick, popsicle, or a loaf of bread.

baudroie monkfish; see *lotte*. *Baudroie* is also a fish stew.

bavarois rich custard dessert made with whipped cream, gelatin and flavorings. Also called *crème bavaroise*.

bavette skirt steak.

béarnaise sauce made with egg yolk, butter, white wine, vinegar, shallots, chervil and tarragon.

Beaufort cow's-milk cheese produced in the French Alps.

béchamel white sauce made with flour, butter, milk or cream and nutmeg.

beignet fritter or doughnut.

Foods & Flavors Guide

berlingot hard candy, usually flavored with peppermint.

bêtise mint-flavored candy from the northern city of Cambrai.

bette chard. Also called *blette*.

betterave beet.

beurre butter.

beurre d'arachides peanut butter.

biche venison (*venaison*) from a female deer (doe).

bien cuit (cooked) well-done.

bière beer. Draught beer is *pression*.

bifteck steak, often a thin and inferior cut.

bifteck haché ground beef or a hamburger.

bigorneau periwinkle, a small snail, steamed and served cold.

Bigoton small goat's-milk cheese from the Orléans region.

biologique organic. Also called simply *bio*.

biscotin cookie. Also see *croquant*.

biscotte toasted bread similar to Melba toast, sold commercially in packages.

biscuit cookie, cracker or sponge cake.

biscuit à la cuillère ladyfinger, also called *langue-de-chat*.

bistro casual restaurant or café. Also spelled *bistrot*.

blanc de poulet white meat of a chicken breast. Also called *blanc de volaille*.

blanc d'œuf egg white.

blé wheat.

blé noir buckwheat flour. Buckwheat is not a wheat but a "pseudo-cereal" in the same plant family as rhubarb. It is used often in Brittany, especially in making savory crêpes. Also called *blé de sarrasin* or *farine de sarrasin*.

blette chard. Also called *bette*.

bleu blue. Refers to a variety of blue cheeses produced across France from either raw or pasteurized milk. *Bleu* can also describe food cooked rare.

bœuf beef. Steak may be prepared *saignant* (rare), *à point* (medium) or *bien cuit* (well done).

boisson drink or beverage.

bol bowl. Morning coffee or hot chocolate is usually served at home in a *bol*. A soup bowl is more commonly *une assiette creuse* or, simply, *une assiette*.

bombe frozen dessert made in a rounded mold to look like a bomb.

(à la) bordelaise prepared in the style of the Bordeaux region, with wine, mushrooms, vegetables and a garnish of artichokes and potatoes.

botte bunch or bundle, usually of vegetables.

bouchée a bite-size puff pastry shell, baked and filled with any number of fillings. Also called *vol-au-vent*.

boucherie butcher shop. A *boucherie chevaline* sells horsemeat.

bouchon cork. Also a casual restaurant, particularly in Lyon, that serves traditional dishes.

boudeuse small oyster, just over an ounce.

boudin type of sausage. *Boudin blanc* is stuffed with poultry, veal and pork. *Boudin noir* is blood sausage made of pork.

bouffe slang term for food.

boulangerie bakery. A *boulangerie* sells bread and rolls; a *pâtisserie* sells pastry and fancy desserts. Very often, one shop offers both.

boule ball or scoop, as of sorbet; a round loaf of bread; or a meatball.

boulette small meatball.

bouquet garni a small bundle of herbs (usually sprigs of parsley, thyme and bay leaf) tied together and used in cooking soups and stews.

(à la) bourgeoise prepared in a style featuring large pieces of braised meat garnished with carrots, onions and bacon.

(à la) bourguignonne prepared in the style of Burgundy, featuring red wine, mushrooms and onions.

Boursin a soft, processed industrial cheese.

bouteille bottle.

brasserie restaurant or café serving food and drinks.

brebis sheep. Also the name given to some ewe's-milk cheeses.

brème bream.

(à la) bretonne prepared in the style of Brittany, including dishes garnished with white beans or incorporating carrots, celery and leeks.

brick phyllo dough.

Brie cow's-milk cheese with a creamy consistency and velvety-white rind.

Brillat-Savarin particularly creamy cow's-milk cheese produced in Normandy, named after French gastronome Jean-Anthelme Brillat-Savarin.

Brin d'Amour Corsican ewe's-milk cheese.

brioche egg and yeast roll or cake. The small *brioche à tête* (with a knob or head) is the most common, but you may also see the larger, crown-shaped *brioche en couronne*.

Brocciu fresh cheese from Corsica, made from the whey of goat's or ewe's milk, and similar to ricotta. Also called *Broccio*.

(à la) broche on a skewer, or spit-roasted.

brochet pike, a long-bodied freshwater fish with firm, white flesh.

brochettes kebabs or bite-sized pieces of meat, fish, poultry or vegetables grilled on a skewer.

brouillade scrambled egg dish with truffles or other ingredients.

brûlé burned, but also caramelized.

brunoise small, diced vegetables.

brut dry, with reference to champagne or cider.

bûche de Noël traditional Christmas sponge cake or Yule log, filled with buttercream.

bugne fritter dusted with confectioners' sugar, a specialty of Lyon.

bulot variety of marine snail or whelk.

Cabécou small goat's-milk cheese from southern France.

cabillaud fresh cod, fished in the North Atlantic.

cabri young goat or kid.

cacahuètes prepared peanuts, for snacking.

café establishment that serves coffee, light meals and snacks. It also means espresso coffee, or *un express*.

café allongé espresso that takes longer to draw from the machine, making the brew weaker.

café américain American-style filtered coffee.

café au lait espresso coffee with milk, more commonly called *un crème*.

café complet coffee with bread, butter and jam or with a morning pastry, such as a croissant.

café décaféiné decaffeinated coffee, also simply *un déca*.

café filtre coffee brewed in a filter or French press.

café liègeois a coffee and ice-cream drink, topped with whipped cream.

café serré especially strong espresso.

cafetière coffee maker.

cagouille kind of snail from the Atlantic coast.

caille quail.

caillette round pork or lamb sausage.

calamar squid.

calisson diamond-shaped candy or cookie, filled with almond paste.

Calvados apple brandy from the Calvados district in Normandy.

Camembert cow's-milk cheese with white mold rind and creamy interior. Its name comes from the eponymous village in Normandy where it is made.

campagne country-style or rustic.

canard duck. *Canard laqué* is glazed or Peking duck.

caneton young male duck.

canneberge cranberry.

cannelé bite-sized chewy French cake, made from a crêpe batter and baked in a fluted mold. It is a specialty of Bordeaux, but found elsewhere.

cannelle cinnamon.

Cantal large cow's-milk cheese from the Auvergne.

carbonnade braised beef stew, cooked with beer and onions.

cardon cardoon or artichoke thistle. This vegetable has stalks that look like celery, but taste like artichokes. Also called *chardon*.

cari curry. Also spelled *cary*.

carré square-shaped, as in a cut of meat or a cheese.

carrelet plaice, a flatfish, distinguishable by its orange-colored markings.

carte menu or list.

carvi caraway. Caraway seeds are *grains de carvi*.

casher Kosher. Also spelled *kasher*.

casse-croûte snack.

cassis black currant, used to make a liqueur (*crème de cassis*) and a syrup (*sirop de cassis*).

cassolette small ovenproof dish, often used to serve appetizers or desserts, or the food itself.

cassonade brown sugar.

cave wine cellar.

céleri-rave celeriac or celery root.

cèpe porcini or small, brown mushroom.

cerf stag.

cerfeuil chervil.

cerise cherry.

cerneau walnut meat.

cervelas cooked sausage made with pork, beef and spices.

cervelles calf's brains.

cévenole prepared in the style of the Cévennes region, with chestnuts or mushrooms.

céviche seviche, raw fish marinated in lime or lemon juice.

Chabichou goat's-milk cheese, produced in a variety of shapes and sizes.

chair meat or flesh.

champignon mushroom.

Chaource soft cow's-milk cheese from the Champagne district.

chapelure breadcrumbs.

chapon capon, or young, castrated and fattened cock.

chapon de mer scorpion fish. See *rascasse*.

charcuterie cooked or cured meats, usually pork, or a store that sells them.

chardon cardoon or artichoke thistle. See *cardon*.

Charolais breed of cattle or a cheese from the Charolais region of Burgundy.

111

Chartreuse green- or yellow-colored liqueur flavored with herbal extracts, once produced by Carthusian monks at the charterhouse in the Alpine Chartreuse mountains but now made nearby under monastic supervision.

Chasselas pale-colored variety of grape, noted for its delicate, sweet flavor. It is eaten as a dessert and used in wine production.

châtaigne chestnut.

Chateaubriand top-quality steak.

chaud hot.

chaud-froid cooked dish, served cold, covered with a sauce and aspic.

chausson sweet or savory turnover.

chemise refers to food served in its own skin, wrapped in pastry or coated with sauce or aspic.

chèvre goat. A *chevreau* is a baby goat or kid.

chevreuil roe deer or venison. Also called *venaison*.

chiboust pastry cream with whipped cream added.

chicon endive.

chicorée chicory or curly endive. Also called *frisée*.

chipiron small squid. Also called *encornet*.

chocolat chocolate. It can be bittersweet (*amer*), milk (*au lait*) or dark (*noir*).

chocolat chaud hot chocolate.

chope mug of beer.

choron béarnaise sauce with tomatoes added.

chou cabbage.

chou à la crème cream puff. An unfilled cream puff is a *chouquette*.

chou de Bruxelles Brussels sprouts, also called *petit chou* or "small cabbage."

chou frisé kale.

chou rouge red cabbage.

choucroute sauerkraut.

chou-fleur cauliflower.

chou-rave kohlrabi.

ciboulette chives.

cidre cider. In France, cider is alcoholic. Apple juice is *jus de pomme*.

citron lemon.

citron pressé fresh-squeezed lemon juice, usually served with water.

citron vert lime. Also called *limon*.

citrouille pumpkin. Also called *potiron* or *potimarron*.

clou de girofle clove. Also simply called *girofle*.

cochon pig. *Cochon de lait* is suckling pig.

cochonnaille pork sausage or other pork product.

cocotte small casserole, in which a dish can be cooked and served.

cœur heart. The word can refer to the actual organ, the center of a vegetable or fruit (as in *cœurs de palmier*, hearts of palm), or a heart-shaped dish (as in *cœurs à la crème*, a sweet cheese dessert served with fruit).

coing quince.

Cointreau orange-flavored liqueur.

colin hake, a flaky white fish in the cod family. A related fish, *merlu*, is sometimes sold as *colin*.

collation light meal.

colza rapeseed oil.

complet full, with no more room.

compris included, such as tax, tip or a drink.

Comté firm, ivory-colored cow's-milk cheese from eastern France.

concombre cucumber.

confiserie candy or candy shop.

confit meat conserved by cooking in its own fat. Also refers to tender, slow-cooked fruits or vegetables that are sometimes candied.

confiture jam.

congre conger eel, a large ocean fish. It is usually cooked in soups and stews.

copeau shaving, as of cheese or chocolate.

coq strictly speaking, a cock or rooster, not a chicken.

coque cockle.

coquillage shellfish. *Coquille Saint-Jacques* means scallop.

corail coral, the delicate orange-colored ovary of a lobster or scallop.

corne horn. *Corne de gazelle* is a crescent-shaped pastry; *corne d'abondance* is a trumpet-shaped mushroom.

cornet cone-shaped food, usually an ice-cream cone.

cornichon small pickle or gherkin.

corsé full-flavored, such as wine or coffee.

côte rib or chop.

couche layer or coating.

coulis juices that run out of cooked meats, but more usually a soup or purée.

Coulommiers type of Brie cheese.

coupe cup, usually filled with fruits, ice cream or champagne.

courbine large bass from the Atlantic or Mediterranean.

courge squash. *Courgette* is zucchini.

couronne crown, usually with reference to bread or pastry.

court-bouillon cooking stock or broth.

couteau knife. *Couteau* also means a razor clam.

couvert place setting.

crème cream, but it may also refer to a variety of foods where cream is used in the dish's preparation. *Café au lait* is sometimes referred to as *un crème*.

crème bavaroise rich custard dessert. See *bavarois*.

crème chantilly sweetened whipped cream.

crème chiboust pastry filling with vanilla and beaten egg white or whipped cream added.

crème de marrons sweetened chestnut purée.

crème fraîche cream soured with bacterial cultures.

crème pâtissière pastry cream.

cremolata frozen juice and syrup concoction similar to sherbet, but may also refer to fish or meat dishes with minced parsley, garlic and lemon zest.

crépinette small sausage patty wrapped in caul fat, the fatty membrane surrounding an animal's internal organs.

cresson watercress.

crevette shrimp, either gray (*grise*) or pink (*rose*).

cristoffine chayote. Also spelled *cristophine*.

croissant crescent-shaped roll, traditionally eaten at breakfast, made with butter (*croissant beurre*) or other fats (*croissant ordinaire*).

croquant cookie. Also called *biscotin*. *Croquant* also means crispy.

crottin small, round goat cheese, sold at various stages of maturity.

croustillant crunchy.

croûte crust. *Croûte de sel* is a salt crust.

cru raw. The term also refers to wine, as in *grand cru*, "a good vintage."

crustacés shellfish.

cuillère spoon.

cuisse thigh or leg.

cuisson cooking, as in time or manner. When waiters say, *"Quelle cuisson?"* they are asking how well-done you want your meat (or fish) cooked.

cuit cooked.

darne fish steak.

datte date.

daube casserole or stew. A *daubière* is an earthenware casserole dish.

daurade sea bream, similar to porgy. Also called *dorade royale*.

décaféiné decaffeinated. Decaffeinated coffee is sometimes referred to simply as *un déca*.

décortiqué shelled.

découpé cut up.

déglacé defrosted. *Déglacé* is also the cooking technique of deglazing a pan.

dégustation tasting, usually with reference to wine.

déjeuner lunch.

délice a delight, a special dish.

demi half, also half bottle (of wine or beer).

demi-sel lightly salted, as in butter.

dénoyauté pitted.

dés dice, as in cut into small cubes.

désossé boned.

diabolo menthe lemonade with mint syrup.

digestif after-dinner (alcoholic) drink.

dinde turkey. Also called *dindonneau*.

dîner dinner.

dorade generic name for a group of ocean fish similar to porgy, such as *dorade grise* (or *griset*), *dorade marbré* (or *marbré*), *dorade rose* (or *pageot rose*) and *dorade royale* or *daurade*.

doré browned or glazed, a golden color.

dos back.

douillon pear baked in a pastry crust, a specialty of Normandy.

doux (douce) soft or sweet.

dragée icing-covered hazelnut or almond, a candy.

dur hard or hard-boiled.

duxelles finely chopped mushrooms, onions and shallots, sautéed in butter and mixed with cream.

eau water.

eau gazeuse carbonated or soda water.

eau minérale mineral water, either fizzy or flat.

eau plate flat mineral water or tap (*robinet*) water.

eau-de-vie liqueur or spirits.

écaillé scaled or opened, as in fish or shellfish.

échalote shallot.

échine chine or loin.

écorce bark or peel.

écrasé crushed, mashed.

écrevisse freshwater crayfish.

effilé thinly sliced. *Effiloché* is shredded.

Foods & Flavors Guide

églefin haddock. Also spelled *aiglefin*.

émincé thin slice of meat or poultry.

Emmental Swiss-style cow's-milk cheese from several regions across France.

emporter to carry out, as in "take-out" food.

encornet small squid. Also called *chipiron*.

encre (squid) ink.

endive Belgian endive.

entrecôte rib steak.

entrée appetizer or first course.

entremet small dish between courses.

épais(se) thick.

épaule shoulder.

épeautre spelt, an ancient and hardy wheat.

éperlan smelt.

épi ear of corn, or bread in the shape of a cornstalk.

épice spice. *Épicé* menas spicy.

épicerie grocery store.

épinard spinach.

Époisses creamy cow's-milk cheese with a soft red rind, from Burgundy.

escalope thin slice of meat or fish.

escargot snail. For more about different types of snails, see p. 30.

espadon swordfish.

Espelette red pepper grown around the French Basque town Espelette. The dried pepper is used as a spice, *piment d'Espelette*.

esqueixada shredded, in the Catalan language. *Esqueixada* also refers to a shredded salt cod salad.

estaminet in northern France, the name for a *bistro* or casual eatery.

estouffade stewed or stuffed dish.

estragon tarragon.

étouffé steamed or braised. Also referred to as *à l'étuvé*.

étrille blue crab.

express espresso coffee.

facturé billed; included in the tab.

faisan pheasant.

faisselle fresh milk cheese, eaten with a spoon.

far a cake-like pudding or flan, a specialty of Brittany but found elsewhere.

farandole (de desserts) a lively choice of desserts. The name comes from a Provençal dance.

farce stuffing.

farcidure fried potato cake. *Farcidure* is also stuffed cabbage.

farine flour. Corn flour is *farine de maïs*; rye flour, *farine de seigle*; whole wheat flour, *farine de blé*; buckwheat flour, *farine de sarrasin* (also called *farine de blé noir*); bran flour, *farine de son*.

fauve wild.

faux-filet sirloin steak.

fécule starch.

fenouil fennel.

fermier farm-fresh, or from a farm (*ferme*).

feu fire; wood fire.

feuille de chêne oak leaf lettuce.

feuilletée referring to puff pastry.

fève fava bean.

fiadone Corsican flan.

ficelle loaf of French bread, thinner and lighter than a *baguette* (a "string").

fin fine or thin.

financier small, rectangular cake.

fine de claire oyster of intermediate saltiness. See p. 27 for more on oysters.

fines herbes mix of fresh herbs, usually chervil, chives, parsley and tarragon.

flageolet small white dried bean.

(à la) flamande prepared in the Flemish style, with cabbage, potatoes and root crops.

flamusse cake or pudding usually made with apples.

flétan halibut.

fleurette pasteurized cream.

flocon flake.

florentine refers to any dish made with spinach.

flûte champagne glass. A *flûte* is also a long loaf of bread, thinner than a *baguette* but fatter than a *ficelle*.

foie liver.

fond cooking stock or juice. The term can also refer to the center or heart of a food.

fondant filling or icing used in pastry making. Fondant also describes moist, gooey desserts. *Moelleux* has a similar meaning.

(à la) forestière prepared with a garnish of morels, ham or bacon, and diced, fried potatoes.

fouace foccacia-type bread. See *fougasse*.

fouetté beaten or whipped.

fougasse foccacia-type bread, often associated with the south of France but found elsewhere. In Provence, the bread is characterized by long slashes or holes in the dough. Also called variously *fouace*, *fouaisse* or *foisse*.

four oven.

fourchette fork.

Fourme from the old French word for cheese, a mild blue cheese made from cow's milk in the Rhône-Alpes and Auvergne regions.

fourré stuffed or filled.

frais (fraîche) fresh.

fraisage process of kneading dough.

fraise strawberry. *Fraise des bois* means wild strawberry but these are usually cultivated. They are smaller than the garden-variety strawberry.

framboise raspberry.

frangipane almond paste.

friand small meat pie.

friandise small pastry or sweet.

fricassée fricasee, meaning braised in white sauce or butter.

frisée curly endive. Also called *chicorée*.

frit fried. French fries are *frites*.

friture fried food. It may also refer to small fried fish, such as smelt.

froid cold.

fromage cheese. France produces more than 200 types of cheeses made from cow's, ewe's or goat's milk. For more on French cheeses, see p. 22.

fromage blanc fresh cow's-milk cheese. Also called *fromage frais* (see *Menu Guide*).

froment wheat.

fruits de mer seafood.

fumé smoked.

fumet fish stock.

galantine meat, usually poultry, that is boned, then stuffed and cooked.

galette pancake, crêpe, cookie, or other round, flat cake.

gamba large shrimp.

ganache chocolate sauce made with cream, used to fill or cover cakes.

garçon obsolete term for waiter (literally, "boy"). *Monsieur* or *Mademoiselle* are the preferred terms. *Serveur* (*serveuse*) is another appropriate term for waiter (waitress).

garniture side dish or decoration, such as vegetables or filling.

gastrique boiled-down sauce of vinegar and sugar.

gâteau cake.

gaufre waffle.

gaufrette wafer. The term usually refers to a sweet wafer often served with ice cream, but can describe latticed fried potatoes.

gazeuse fizzy or carbonated, as in *eau gazeuse,* "fizzy water."

gelée jelly or aspic.

genièvre juniper berry.

génoise sponge cake.

germe kernel or sprout.

gésier gizzard.

gibassier sweet bread made with olive oil, a specialty of Provence.

gibier game.

gigot roast, usually leg of lamb.

gingembre ginger.

girofle clove. Also called *clou de girofle.*

girolle golden chanterelle, a pale-orange or deep-yellow wild mushroom.

givré frosted. It also refers to orange sorbet served in the fruit's skin.

glaçage frosting.

glace ice or ice cream.

glacé covered with sugar or frosted.

glacier ice-cream shop or ice-cream maker.

glaçon ice cube.

godet small dish or ramekin.

gombo okra. Also spelled *gombaut.*

goujon small catfish or other small fish.

gousse clove or bean, such as garlic or vanilla.

goût taste. *Goûter* can refer to an afternoon tea or snack.

goutte drop.

goyave guava.

grain bean or grain, such as *grain de café,* "coffee bean."

graisse fat.

grand cru top-ranked wine.

grappe bunch.

gras(grasse) fat or fatty.

gratinée onion soup, topped with grated cheese. Also, having a browned top.

gratton pork crackling.

FOODS & FLAVORS GUIDE

gratuit without charge, free.

grenade pomegranate.

grenouille frog. Frog's legs are *cuisses de grenouille*.

gribiche vinaigrette with hard-boiled eggs, capers, herbs and small pickles.

grillé grilled. *Grillade* is grilled meat.

griotte cherry.

griottine small Morello cherry macerated in Kirsch liqueur.

grondin gurnard, a flavorful but bony saltwater fish that is either red or gray in color. It is similar to a sea robin, and used mostly in soups.

gros(se) thick.

groseille red or white currant.

groseille à maquereau gooseberry.

Gruyère generic name for Swiss-style cheeses, from the name of the town in Switzerland.

guimauve marshmallow.

haché chopped.

hachis hash.

hareng herring.

haricot bean, such as *haricot vert* or green bean.

harissa North African hot chile paste.

herbes de Provence blend of dried herbs that may include basil, fennel, lavender, rosemary, savory and thyme.

hérisson chocolate mousse or cake covered with chocolate, dusted with cocoa, and sometimes spiked with nuts, so called because it is shaped to resemble a hedgehog (*hérisson*).

hollandaise sauce made of butter, eggs and lemon juice.

homard lobster.

huile oil.

huîtres oysters, usually served raw. (Be advised that eating raw or undercooked foods may increase the risk of food-borne illness.) The menu will usually indicate how many to an order. For more about different types of oysters, see p. 27.

igname yam.

imprégné steeped or soaked.

inclus included, such as tax and tip on a restaurant bill. Also *compris*.

infusion herbal tea, usually mint, chamomile, linden or vervain Also called *tisane*.

jalousie puff pastry filled with almond paste or jam.

jambon ham. *Jambonneau* is cured ham shank or knuckle.

(à la) jardinière prepared with a garnish of fresh vegetables, cooked separately, arranged around a main dish. A garden is *un jardin*.

jarret beef, veal or pork knuckle, or shin of beef.

jaune d'œuf egg yolk.

joue jowl or cheek.

judru short, stubby sausage from Burgundy.

julienne very thinly sliced vegetables. *Julienne* is also ling, a fish in the cod family.

jus juice. The word can refer to fruit juices as well as liquid from foodstuffs, including vegetables, meats or poultry.

juteux (juteuse) juicy.

kaki persimmon.

kasher Kosher. Also spelled *casher*.

kir aperitif made with white wine and black currant syrup. The drink is called *kir royal* if made with champagne.

kougloff cake made with yeast dough and dried fruit. Also called *kugelhopf,* a specialty of the Alsace region.

kouing amman buttery cake from Brittany.

lait milk. *Laitier* means made from or with milk.

lait concentré condensed milk.

lait cru raw milk.

lait écrémé skim milk.

lait en poudre powdered milk.

lait entier whole milk.

lait ribot buttermilk.

laitue lettuce.

lamproie lamprey eel.

langouste rock lobster or crayfish. Unlike lobster, it has no claws.

langoustine member of the lobster family about the size of a shrimp, but with a wider tail and claws.

langue-de-chat ladyfinger. Also called *biscuit à la cuillère*.

lapin rabbit. A young rabbit is a *lapereau*.

lard fatback or slab bacon. *Lardon* is a small strip or cube of bacon.

lard de poitrine bacon.

laurier bay leaf.

léger light.

légume vegetable.

lentille lentil. The green Le Puy lentil from the Auvergne is especially prized.

levain bread-leavening agent, such as a sourdough starter.

levure yeast.

levure chimique baking powder.

liaison thickening.

(à la) liègeoise prepared in the style of Liège, with juniper flavoring.

lieu noir pollock, a fish in the cod family.

lièvre hare.

limande lemon sole, a flatfish similar to flounder but more elongated and oval, fished in the North Atlantic.

limon lime. Also called *citron vert*.

limoux sparkling white wine.

lingue ling, a fish in the cod family.

lisette mackerel. The saltwater fish is usually broiled. Also called *maquereau*.

lit bed or layer.

Livarot strong-flavored cow's-milk cheese from the eponymous village in Normandy. The cheese has strips of raffia tied around it, and these stripes have earned it the nickname "the Colonel."

livèche lovage, an herb in the angelica family.

lotte monkfish or angler fish, a firm-fleshed saltwater fish with a particularly ugly face, which is usually cut off. Also called *baudroie*.

loup sea bass. Also called *loup de mer* and *bar*.

louquenka Basque sausage made with garlic and chile pepper.

lunettes Linzer-like tartlet with two holes (like "eye glasses") revealing a jam filling.

(à la) lyonnaise prepared in the style of the Lyon region, cooked with onions.

macédoine diced vegetables or fruits.

mâche small-leaved, nutty salad green.

macis mace.

(à la) maconnaise prepared in the style of the Macon region, with red or white wine.

madeleine small sponge cake in the shape of a shell.

magret breast of duck or other meat.

maigre thin, lean.

maïs corn.

maison refers to a restaurant ("house") or food that is homemade.

maître d'hôtel head waiter or house manager. May also refer to a sauce of butter, lemon juice and parsley.

mandoline slicing machine.

manié kneaded or worked.

maquereau mackerel. The saltwater fish is usually broiled. Also called *lisette*.

maraîchère refers to a dish served with braised mixed vegetables.

marbré marbled.

marc kind of brandy made from pressed grape skins.

marcassin young wild boar.

marchand de vin sauce from red wine, meat stock and shallots.

marinière refers to a dish cooked in white wine and shallots.

marjolaine marjoram. It is also the name of a chocolate nut cake.

marmite saucepan or casserole, as well as the food cooked in it.

Maroilles robust cow's-milk cheese from the eponymous northern French town. Also spelled Marolle.

marquise sponge cake. It is also a variety of tender, sweet pear.

marron chestnut.

massepain marzipan.

matefaim thick pancake that may have sweet or savory fillings.

matelote fish stew.

mélasse molasses.

méli-mélo seafood or fish medley. Also a mixed-fruit dish.

mendiant candy or dessert made with dried fruit and nuts.

merguez spicy sausage made from beef, lamb or both meats.

merlan whiting, a northern saltwater fish with delicate flesh.

merlu hake, a flaky white fish in the cod family. *Merlu* is often sold as *colin*, another fish in the cod family.

mérou grouper.

mets general term that refers to food prepared for the table.

meunière in the style of the miller's wife, meaning dishes that are lightly floured and sautéed in butter, then served with lemon and parsley.

meurette refers to dishes with a red-wine sauce, such as *œufs en meurette*, a Burgundian specialty.

mie de pain crumb.

miel honey.

mignardise small pastry or cookie, served at the end of a meal.

mignonette coarsely ground pepper, or small cubes of beef.

Foods & Flavors Guide

mijoté simmered.

mille-feuille layers of puff pastry with a sweet or savory filling.

millésime the vintage year of a wine, marked on the bottle label and cork.

Mimolette large, orange-colored cow's-milk cheese, similar to Dutch Edam, produced in northern France.

mimosa garnished with hard-boiled eggs.

minard octopus. Also called *poulpe* and *pieuvre*.

mirabelle type of small plum, golden in color.

mirepoix diced carrots, celery and onions, added to sauces or used in the preparation of particular dishes.

mirliton small tartlet, a specialty of Rouen.

miroir baked in the oven or glazed to give a mirror-like film, as in the baked egg dish *œufs miroir*.

(à la) mode in the manner of.

moelle marrow.

moelleux describes desserts that are moist and gooey. *Fondant* has a similar meaning.

mollet soft, often with reference to an egg dish.

Mont-d'Or orange-colored cheese, made from goat's and cow's milk in central and eastern France.

monter refers to cooking technique where butter is whipped into a sauce to lift or thicken it.

Morbier cow's-milk cheese from the Jura, recognizable by its distinctive blue-gray ribbon of ash.

morille wild morel mushroom.

Mornay béchamel sauce enhanced with egg yolks and cheese.

morue salt cod. *Morue fraîche* is cod.

moule mussel. *Moule* is also a mold used to give food a decorative shape.

moulu ground.

mousseline hollandaise sauce lightened with whipped cream.

mousseux (mousseuse) frothy.

moutarde mustard.

mulard breed of duck, found in the southwest.

mulet mullet. Not to be confused with red mullet, or *rouget*.

Munster soft cow's-milk cheese with reddish rind from eastern France.

mûr ripe.

mûre blackberry.

muscade nutmeg.

myrtille blueberry. Also called *airelle*.

(à la) nage method of cooking or poaching shellfish in broth.

Nantua classic seafood cream sauce.

nappe tablecloth.

nappé covered with a sauce or syrup.

natte braided bread.

nature plain, simple, without additional ingredients.

navarin mutton or lamb stew.

navet turnip.

nem spring roll.

Neufchâtel creamy, heart-shaped cow's-milk cheese from Normandy.

(à la) niçoise prepared Nice-style, with olives, garlic, anchovies and tomatoes.

nid edible nest-like construction, such as is made with matchstick potatoes.

noisette hazelnut. *Noisette* is also a small, round piece of meat, or a knob of butter (*noisette de beurre*).

noix walnut. Also refers to nuts generally.

noix de beurre nut-sized piece of butter. Also *noisette de beurre*.

noix de cajou cashew.

non compris not included, such as a tip.

nonette small, round gingerbread cake, a specialty of the Burgundy region.

nonpareille capers pickled in vinegar. It is also a colored granulated sugar used in decorating, or a variety of pear.

(à la) normande prepared Normandy-style, with cream, cider and apples.

note the bill. Also called *l'addition*.

nouilles noodles.

nouveau (nouvelle) new.

noyau stone or pit.

œuf egg. For particular egg dishes, see *Menu Guide*, p. 93.

oie goose.

omble char or lake fish.

onglet flank steak.

oreille ear.

orge barley.

orgeat sweet beverage made with ground almonds.

ormeau abalone.

ortie nettle.

oseille sorrel.

oursin sea urchin.

FOODS & FLAVORS GUIDE

pagaille mixture or hash.

pageot pandora fish, similar to porgy, usually broiled or fried. See *dorade*.

paille straw.

pain bread. See entries below as well as *baguette*, *bâtard*, *boule*, *ficelle*, *flûte* and *fougasse*.

pain au chocolat small pastry filled with chocolate.

pain au lait bread or roll made with milk.

pain complet whole-wheat bread.

pain de campagne country-style or rustic loaf.

pain de mie white bread.

pain de seigle rye bread.

pain de son bran bread.

pain d'épices spice cake or gingerbread.

pain grillé grilled bread or toast.

pain perdu French toast.

paleron shoulder of beef.

palmiers palm-shaped puff pastry cookie.

palourde medium-sized clam.

pamplemousse grapefruit.

panaché mixed or mixture; a beer mixed with soda water.

panais parsnip.

pané breaded.

panisse savory fried snack made with chickpea flour.

pannequet sweet or savory pancake.

papillon small oyster. See p. 27 for more on different types of oysters.

(en) papillotte cooked in parchment paper.

parfum flavor.

parmentier describes any dish with potatoes as a main ingredient.

passoir sieve.

pastèque watermelon.

pastille small, round sugar candies.

pastis anise-flavored aperitif.

pâte dough or paste. Also means pasta.

pâté forcemeat, or meat or fish spread, sometimes baked in a crust or in a special baking dish called a *terrine*.

pâte à chou chou or cream puff paste made of water or milk, butter, flour and eggs.

pâte brisée short pastry.

pâte feuilletée puff pastry.

pâte sucrée sweetened short pastry.

pâtisserie pastry or pastry shop.

paupiette thin slice of meat or fish fillet stuffed with forcemeat, then rolled and cooked.

pavé thick piece of meat, shaped like a paving stone. The term can also refer to a square-shaped sponge cake as well as a cheese.

pavot poppy seed.

(à la) paysanne prepared country-style, with meats braised and garnished with root crops.

peau skin.

pêche peach.

pélardon small, pungent goat's-milk cheeses from south central France.

perche perch, a freshwater fish.

perdreau partridge. Also called *perdrix*.

(à la) périgourdine prepared in the style of the Périgord region, with truffles or sometimes poultry liver.

persillade seasoning or garnish of chopped parsley, garlic and shallots added to dishes at the end of cooking.

persillé covered with parsley. Also refers to certain blue-veined cheeses.

pépite nugget or small piece.

petit beurre small butter cookie.

petit déjeuner breakfast ("small meal").

petit gris type of snail most typically raised in France.

petit pois green pea.

pétoncle small scallop.

pichet pitcher.

Picodon small goat's-milk cheese from the Rhône region.

pied-de-mouton hedgehog mushroom. This wild mushroom is named in French for the shape of the cap (like a sheep's foot). The English name (hedgehog) refers to the spines on the underside of the cap.

pieds et paquets mutton tripe cooked with sheep's feet, a specialty of southern France.

pieuvre octopus. Also called *poulpe* and *minard*.

pignon de pin pine nut.

piment pimento or red pepper.

piment d'Espelette spice from dried red pepper grown around the French Basque town Espelette, similar to paprika.

pince claw; tongs.

pintade guinea hen, a flavorful bird leaner than chicken.

pissenlit dandelion green.

pistou pesto-like spread made of basil, garlic, olive oil and sometimes Parmesan cheese.

Pithiviers puff pastry cake filled with almond paste, a specialty of Pithiviers. Also a cow's-milk cheese from the same area.

plaisir a small wafer.

plat dish. *Plat du jour* is the daily special.

plateau tray or platter.

pleurote oyster mushroom, both wild and cultivated.

poché poached.

poêle frying pan or skillet. Fried dishes are often referred to as *poêlé(e)*.

pogne sweet yeast bread, a specialty of east central France. *Pogne* may also refer to a squash pie.

(à) point refers to meat cooked medium-rare. Also means ripe.

pointe tip or end.

poire pear.

poireau leek.

pois pea.

pois chiche chickpea.

poisson fish. A *poissonnerie* is a fish shop.

poisson-chat catfish.

poitrine breast.

poivre pepper. *Poivrade* is a peppery brown sauce.

poivron green, red or yellow pepper.

pomme apple.

pomme de terre potato. Also called *patate*.

Pont-L'Évêque cow's-milk cheese from Normandy—one of France's oldest.

porc pork. *Porcelet* is suckling pig.

Port-Salut cow's-milk cheese from the Pays de la Loire in western France.

pot-au-feu beef stew.

potage soup.

potager kitchen garden.

potée meat and vegetable stew, with many variations, traditionally cooked in an earthenware pot.

potiron pumpkin. Also called *potimarron* and *citrouille*.

poularde fattened chicken.

poule chicken. Also *poulet*. A *poulet fermier* is a farm-raised chicken.

poulpe octopus. Also called *pieuvre* and *minard*.

pourpier purslane, a succulent plant used in salads and soups.

pousse shoot, as in bamboo shoot, *pousse de bambou*.

poussin baby chicken.

praire small clam.

pressé squeezed. It can also mean in a hurry.

pression draft beer.

primeurs first vegetables and fruits of spring.

printanier a mixture of vegetables cut into dice or diamond shapes and cooked separately, then served as a garnish with a main dish.

prix fixe fixed-price menu.

prix nets service (tip) included.

profiterole classic dessert made from chou paste with a sweet filling, such as custard, pastry cream, whipped cream or ice cream. It is often topped with chocolate sauce.

(à la) provençale prepared in the style of Provence in southern France, with olive oil, garlic and tomatoes.

prune plum.

pruneau prune.

prunelle sloe, a tiny plum.

puits d'amour jam- or custard-filled puff pastry cakes—"wells of love."

quart a quarter or fourth.

quasi veal loin.

quatre épices spice mix, usually cloves, ginger, nutmeg and pepper.

quenelle poached dumpling of fish, poultry or meat mousse. *Quenelle* may refer to foods such as ice cream or mashed potatoes shaped in an oval.

quetsche purple plum.

queue tail.

rabiole rutabaga.

râble saddle of meat.

racine root.

Raclette cow's-milk cheese, similar to Swiss cheese. See *Menu Guide* for the dish of the same name.

ragoût stew.

raie skate or ray, a fish found along the North Sea and English Channel.

raifort horseradish.

raisin grape. A *raisin sec* is a raisin.

râpé grated.

rascasse scorpion fish, a saltwater fish from the Mediterranean with firm white flesh. *Rascasse* is also called *chapon de mer.*

ratafia liqueur infused with nuts or fruit.

ratte small potato.

ravigote classic white sauce, highly seasoned, and used either warm or cold.

Reblochon rich and nutty cow's-milk cheese from eastern France.

recette recipe.

réchauffé reheated.

réglisse licorice.

religieuse pastry made of chou paste, filled with pastry cream and covered with glaze.

remonter culinary term meaning to add an ingredient to a sauce or dish to lift or strengthen its flavor.

remoulade mayonnaise-like sauce including pickles, capers, scallions and herbs.

repas meal.

requin shark.

revenir culinary term meaning to brown ingredients in butter or fat.

rillettes meat, poultry or fish spread.

ris sweetbreads, the thymus or pancreas of an animal, usually lamb or veal.

rissolé deep-fat fried.

riz rice.

rognon kidney.

romarin rosemary.

Roquefort ewe's-milk blue cheese ripened in caves in Roquefort-sur-Soulzon in southern France.

roquette arugula or rocket, a salad green.

rosette type of sausage, a specialty of the area around Lyon.

roseval small, red-skinned potato.

rôti roasted or a roast.

rouget red mullet. This fish has fine white flesh and is usually grilled or fried.

rougette red-leafed butter lettuce, a specialty of Provence.

rouille mayonnaise sauce made of saffron, garlic, olive oil and fish broth.

roulade rolled meat.

roulé rolled. *Gâteau roulé* is a jelly roll.

sabayon thick custard made with egg yolks, sugar, wine and flavorings; from the Italian word *zabaglione.*

sablé cookie or cake, with many variations around the country.

sabodet particularly strong-flavored pork sausage, a specialty of Lyon.

sacristain sweet puff pastry twist.

saignant cooked rare.

Saint-Marcellin small cow's- or goat's-milk cheese from southern France.

Saint-Pierre John Dory or Saint Peter's fish, a saltwater fish.

saisi seared so that the juices are sealed into the flesh.

salade salad. A *saladier* is a salad bowl.

salamandre a grill.

salé salty or salted.

Salers cheese similar to Cantal, produced in the mountains of the Auvergne region with milk from cows pastured during the spring and summer.

salmis classically prepared dish with meat or poultry napped with juices from the pressed carcass.

salon de thé tearoom.

salpicon cooked, diced ingredients used as a filling or stuffing in a variety of either sweet or savory dishes.

salsifis salsify or oyster plant, a root vegetable.

sandre freshwater fish with a delicate taste, similar to pike and perch.

sang blood.

sanglier wild boar.

sarriette the herb savory.

saucisse uncooked sausage. *Saucisson* is cured or smoked sausage.

sauge sage.

saumon salmon.

saupoudré powdered.

sauvage wild.

savarin yeast cake in the shape of a ring or crown, infused with a rum-flavored sugar syrup.

(à la) savoyarde cooked in the style of the Savoie region, featuring potatoes and cheese.

sec (sèche) dry. When used to describe champagne, *sec* means sweet.

seiche cuttlefish, a cephalopod similar to squid.

seigle rye.

sel salt. Sea salt is *fleur de sel*.

selle saddle.

selon according to (size, *poids;* weight, *grosseur;* availability, *marché;* or season, *saison*).

semoule semolina.

seriole amberjack, a type of Atlantic fish in the same family as pompano.

serveur (serveuse) waiter (waitress).

service compris service (tip) included. *Service non compris* means the tip is not included. *Service en sus* means an additional charge.

serviette napkin or towel.

sirop d'érable maple syrup.

snacké food pan-seared or grilled quickly, without (or with very little) fat.

socca round, thin pancake made with chickpea flour, a specialty of Nice.

soin care. On a menu, the term *par nos soins* suggests food is homemade.

soja soy.

sommelier wine steward.

son bran.

soubise purée of onions and rice, a creamy onion sauce or a dish topped with an onion sauce.

souper evening or late-night meal.

soupière soup tureen.

spätzel small dumpling resembling a noodle, a specialty of the Alsace region. Also spelled *spaetzle*.

succès layer cake filled with buttercream.

sucre sugar. *Sucré* means sweetened. A sugar bowl is a *sucrier*.

sucrine lettuce that is similar to both romaine and butter lettuce.

supion small octopus.

suprême white sauce made with butter, cream, flour and chicken stock. It is also a boneless breast of poultry or fish fillet.

surgelé frozen.

table d'hôte serving dinner for residents, guests.

tablette bar of chocolate.

tamis sieve.

tapenade olive spread, including olives, anchovies, capers and olive oil, a specialty of Provence now found across France.

tartare chopped raw meat or fish.

tarte open-faced pie or tart, usually sweet.

tartine lengthwise slice of *baguette*, served with butter and jam for breakfast.

tasse cup.

tastevin special cup for tasting wine.

telline tiny clam found in the Provence and Camargue regions.

terrine earthenware dish used for cooking a dish, or the dish itself.

terroir region or land, referring to local products and regional cooking.

tête head.

thé tea, either black or green. Herbal tea is called *infusion* or *tisane*.

thon tuna.

tian earthenware baking dish or a vegetable stew cooked in a *tian*.

tielle small savory pastry, filled with squid or octopus and tomato, a specialty of the Languedoc-Roussillon.

tige stalk or stem.

tilleul linden tree and the tea brewed from its flowers.

timbale small round mold, or a mixture of custard, forcemeat, vegetables and sometimes other ingredients cooked in the mold.

tire-bouchon corkscrew.

tisane herbal tea, usually mint, chamomile, linden (*tilleul*) or vervain (*verveine*). Also called *infusion*.

tomme variety of round cheeses made across France sometimes made from low-fat cow's, ewe's or goat's milk. Also spelled *tome*.

topinambour Jerusalem artichoke.

torréfié roasted, with particular reference to coffee and chocolate.

tournesol sunflower.

touron type of nougat, made from marzipan, nuts and honey.

tourte pie or tart.

tourteau large crab.

traiteur caterer.

tranche slice.

travers spareribs.

trévise radicchio or bitter red lettuce.

tripe animal intestines and stomach.

triple-crème cheese containing more than 75% butterfat.

trompette de la mort black trumpet, a wild mushroom.

truffe much sought after and very expensive underground fungus. A *truffe* is also a chocolate *bonbon* or truffle.

truite trout.

tuile rounded almond cookie, in the shape of a French roof tile.

vache cow.

Vacherin soft cow's-milk cheese from the Savoie and Franche-Comté. It is also a meringue filled with ice cream, sweetened whipped cream and fruit.

vapeur steamed.

Foods & Flavors Guide

veau veal.

velouté thick cream- or egg-based soup. Also, a white sauce that is the base for other sauces.

venaison venison. Also called *chevreuil*. *Biche* is venison from a female deer.

verdure greens.

vergeoise raw sugar.

verjus acidic juice from unripe grapes, used as vinegar.

verre glass.

vert green or unripe.

verveine vervain, an herbal tea.

viande meat.

viennoise coated with egg or mustard, breaded and fried.

viennoiserie breakfast pastry made with yeast dough and butter.

vierge virgin, or best-quality, such as olive oil. *Vierge* is also a sauce made with butter, lemon juice and pepper.

vigne vine. A vineyard is a *vignoble*.

vin wine.

volaille poultry.

vol-au-vent puff pastry shell, baked and filled with meat, fish or vegetable. Also called *bouchée*, although the latter may be smaller.

Food Establishments

A Quick Reference Guide to Restaurants and Shops Visited

These food establishments were among many that were visited or consulted in researching *Eat Smart in France*. The telephone country code for France is 33. (You must first dial 011 from the US for international calls.) An area code immediately precedes the eight-digit phone number. If you call from outside France, you must use both 33 and the area code, such as 1 for Paris. If you call from France, omit the country code; dial a 0 and the area code.

Restaurants

L'Auberge du Beau-Lieu 2 route du Montadet, 76440 Le Fossé, Forges-les-Eaux   Tel (33) (0) 2 35 90 50 36   aubeaulieu@aol.com www.aubergedubeaulieu.fr

La Cuisine de Bar 8 rue du Cherche-Midi, 75006 Paris Tel (33) (0) 1 45 48 45 69

La Ferme de la Ruchotte 21360 Bligny-sur-Ouche Tel (33) (0) 3 80 20 04 79   http://laruchotte-leblog.blogspot.com

L'Hostellerie du Moulin Fouret 27300 Saint-Aubin-le-Vertueux Tel (33) (0) 2 32 43 19 95   lemoulinfouret@wanadoo.fr www.moulin-fouret.com

Le Piano Qui Fume 36 rue Berbisey, 21000 Dijon Tel (33) (0) 3 80 30 35 45   info@lepianoquifume.fr www.lepianoquifume.fr

Restaurant Stéphane Derbord 10 place Wilson, 21000 Dijon Tel (33) (0) 3 80 67 74 64   www.restaurantstephanederbord.fr

Le Rouennais 5 rue de la Pie, 76000 Rouen   Tel (33) (0) 2 35 07 55 44

Les Routiers 50 bis rue Marx Dormoy, 75018 Paris Tel (33) (0) 1 46 07 93 80

La Terrasse du Mimosa   23 place de l'Horloge, 34150 Montpeyroux
   Tel (33) (0) 4 67 44 49 80   lemimosa@free.fr
   www.laterrassedumimosa.blogspot.com
La Vieille Auberge   15 rue Grillot, 21210 Saulieu
   Tel (33) (0) 3 80 64 13 74   lavieilleauberge3@wanadoo.fr

Shops, Manufacturers and Farms with Sales Areas

Cellier Clos du Bourg (Calvados) 76270 Saint-Saire
   Tel (33) (0) 2 32 97 10 74   http://pagesperso-orange.fr/closdubourg
Christian Constant Chocolatier   37 rue d'Assas, 75006 Paris
   Tel (33) (0) 1 53 63 15 15   christianconstant@orange.fr
   A small café is attached to the pastry and chocolate shop.
La Ferme de Hyaumet (organic Neufchâtel cheese)   76220 Dampierre-en-
   Bray   Tel (33) (0) 6 87 39 29 33
La Ferme de Saint Mamert (organic bread)   32 rue des Glycines, 27240
   Buis-sur-Damville   Tel (33) (0) 6 32 47 42 56
La Grande Duchesse (candies, cookies)   13 rue Castellane, 75008 Paris
   Tel (33) (0) 1 42 66 12 57   www.lagrandeduchesse.com
Huilerie Coopérative de Clermont-l'Hérault   13 avenue du Président
   Wilson, 34800 Clermont-l'Hérault   Tel (33) (0) 4 67 96 10 36
   www.olidoc.com
La Maison Mulot & Petitjean (spice bread)   13 place Bossuet, 21000 Dijon
   Tel (33) (0) 3 80 30 07 10   www.mulotpetitjean.fr
Manoir du Val (Calvados)   27410 Saint-Aubin-le-Guichard
   Tel (33) (0) 23 22 43 45 19   http://manoirduval.free.fr
La Moutarderie Fallot (mustard)   31 rue du Faubourg Bretonnière, 21200
   Beaune   Tel (33) (0) 3 80 22 10 02   info@fallot.com   www.fallot.com
Poilâne (bread, pastries)   8 rue du Cherche-Midi, 75006 Paris
   Tel (33) (0) 1 45 48 42 59   www.poilane.fr

Cooking Schools

At Home With Patricia Wells   www.patriciawells.com
On Rue Tatin Cooking School   www.onruetatin.com
Provence Cooks   www.cuisineprovencale.com

Bibliography

Abramson, Julia. *Food Culture in France*. Westport, CT: Greenwood Press, 2007.

Aussignac, Pascal. *Cuisinier Gascon: Meals from a Gascon Chef*. Bath: Absolute Press, 2009.

Caws, Mary Ann. *Provençal Cooking: Savoring the Simple Life in France*. New York: Pegasus, 2008.

Child, Julia and Alex Prud'homme. *My Life in France*. New York: Anchor Books, 2007.

Curtis, Gregory. *The Cave Painters*. New York: Anchor, 2007.

Dominé, André, editor. *Culinaria France*. Königswinter, Germany: Könemann, 2004.

Drouard, Alain. *Les Français et la table. Alimentation, cuisine, gastronomie du Moyen Âge à nos jours*. Paris: Ellipses, 2005.

Effros, Bonnie. *Creating Community with Food and Drink in Merovingian Gaul*. New York: Palgrave McMillan, 2002.

Fischler, Claude and Estelle Masson. *Manger: Français, Européens et Américains Face à l'Alimentation*. Paris: Odile Jacob, 2008.

Flouest, Anne and Jean-Paul Romac. *La cuisine néolithique et la grotte de La Molle-Pierre*. Paris: Jean-Paul Rocher, 2007.

Freidberg, Susanne. *French Beans and Food Scares: Culture and Commerce in an Anxious Age*. New York: Oxford University Press, 2004.

Graf, Christine and Dennis Graf. *Paris by Bistro: A Guide to Eating Well*. New York: Interlink Books, 2004.

Grescoe, Taras. *Bottomfeeder: How to Eat Ethically in a World of Vanishing Seafood*. New York: Bloomsbury, 2008.

Jefford, Andrew. *The New France: A Complete Guide to Contemporary French Wine*. London: Mitchell Beazley, 2002.

Jones, Colin. *The Great Nation: France from Louis XV to Napoleon*. London: Penguin, 2003.

Kaplan, Steven L. (Catherine Porter, trans.). *Good Bread Is Back: A Contemporary History of French Bread, the Way It Is Made And the People Who Make It*. Durham, North Carolina: Duke University Press, 2006.

Kladstrup, Don and Petie Kladstrup. *Champagne: How the World's Most Glamorous Wine Triumphed Over War and Hard Times*. New York: William Morrow, 2005.

Lobrano, Alexander. *Hungry for Paris: The Ultimate Guide to the City's 102 Best Restaurants*. New York: Random House, 2008.

Long, Dixon and Ruthanne Long. *Markets of Paris*. New York: The Little Bookroom, 2006.

Loomis, Susan Herrmann. *French Farmhouse Cookbook*. New York: Workman, 1996.

Masui, Kazuko and Tomoko Yamada. *French Cheeses*. New York: DK Publishing, 1996.

Mennell, Stephen. *All Manners of Food: Eating and Taste in England and France from the Middle Ages to the Present*. Urbana and Chicago: University of Illinois Press, 1996.

Montagné, Prosper. *The New Larousse Gastronomique*. New York: Crown Publishers, 1977.

Pinkard, Susan. *A Revolution in Taste: The Rise of French Cuisine*. New York: Cambridge University Press, 2009.

Pitte, Jean-Robert. *French Gastronomy: The History and Geography of a Passion*. New York: Columbia University Press, 2002.

Rio, Marie-Noël. *The Food of Paris*. Hong Kong: Periplus Editions, 2002.

Robb, Graham. *The Discovery of France*. New York: W.W. Norton, 2007.

Roberts, Michael. *Parisian Home Cooking*. New York: William Morrow, 1999.

Root, Waverly. *The Food of France*. New York: Alfred A. Knopf, 1973.

Steinberger, Michael. *Au Revoir to All That: Food, Wine and the End of France*. New York: Bloomsbury, 2009.

Tannahill, Reay. *Food in History*. New York: Stein and Day, 1974.

Tilleray, Brigitte. *The Frenchwoman's Kitchen*. London: Seven Dials, 1999.

Toussaint, Jean-Luc (Michael Hinden and Betsy Draine, trans.). *The Walnut Cookbook*. Berkeley: Ten Speed Press, 1998.

Trubek, Amy. *Haute Cuisine: How the French Invented the Culinary Profession*. Philadelphia: University of Pennsylvania Press, 2000.

Trubek, Amy. *The Taste of Place: A Cultural Journey into Terroir*. Berkeley: University of California Press, 2008.

Villegas, Maria and Sarah Randell. *The Food of France: A Journey for Food Lovers*. North Vancouver: Whitecap, 2005.

Wells, Patricia. *Vegetable Harvest*. New York: William Morrow, 2007.

Wheaton, Barbara Ketcham. *Savoring the Past: The French Kitchen Table from 1300 to 1789*. New York: Touchstone, 1996.

Willan, Anne. *The Country Cooking of France*. San Francisco: Chronicle Books, 2007.

Willan, Anne. *Great Cooks and Their Recipes: From Taillevent to Escoffier*. New York: McGraw Hill, 1977.

Woodward, Sarah. *The Food of France: A Regional Celebration*. London: Kyle Books, 2006.

Index

INDEX

140

design   Ekeby
cover design   Susan P. Chwae
color printing   Traver Graphics, Inc.
book production   Sheridan Books, Inc.

typefaces   Garamond Simoncini and Helvetica Black
paper   60# Offset